M000107741

Right Hand to the Champ: 13 Lessons that Changed My Life

By Tasha Robinson-White

With Cassandra Cousineau

Copyright © 2014 by Write Hand Publishing & Entertainment

All Rights Reserved.

No part of this publication may be reproduced, distributed, or transmitted in any form or by any means, including photocopying, recording, or other electronic or mechanical methods, without the prior written permission of the author, except the use of brief quotations for the sole purpose of a book review.

www.righthandtothechamp.com

ISBN: 978-0-692-29654-7

First Printing – December 2014

Proudly Printed in the United States of America

DEDICATION

This Memoir is dedicated to my soldiers in heaven my Father Larry Burnell Robinson, Baby brother Kahil Trameil Robinson, Earon "Papa" Robinson, Grandfather Thomas "Pee Wee" Cannon, Father-in-law Karl Miller...

To my champions on earth Husband Kevin L. White, Son Kevin 'KJ" White and my Brother Lawrence A. Robinson.

Because of your heart, I know the meaning of unconditional love.

ACKNOWLEDGEMENTS

I was reluctant to write this book. I felt vulnerable sharing such a deeply personal story. Having my business out there, so to speak, also cast a spotlight on my family. The only way I found the courage to write this memoir, was through their unconditional support. Without my family, none of this would be possible.

My heartfelt gratitude to my family--

To my loving Mother Willabea Robinson who always has my back no matter what; to my Daughter Jaelin White whose breathtaking beauty on the outside is surpassed by her immeasurable beauty in the inside; to my Nieces Xia & Seniya Robinson who keep the torch lit for their departed father Kahil Robinson; to my Nephews Trey & Tye Robinson the dynamic duo; to the heart and soul of the Robinson family my Grandmother Ludie Mae Robinson; to Godmother Margaret Helen Carter who holds my secrets; to the phenomenal Miss Doris White Miller you've always been more than a Mother-in-law to me; to Mr. Personality my Godson Braxton Selvey; to my Aunts Geraldine, Joyce, Yvonne, Rachel, Cathy, and Beverly who allow me to stand in the circle; to my Uncles Raven and Thomas who personify courage; to my honorary Uncles even though they are my cousins Clyde and Stevie, to my Cousins Juan, Anthony, Daryl, Taurus, Neisha, April, Bonnie, Cody, Michael, Tyra, James, Eon, Chayna, Christopher, DeMychael, Raquel, Mariyah, Brandon, and Tushon; to the Robinson, Parker, White, Miller, Hightower, Hefners, Weeks, and Cannon families-we are one.

~~~~~~

The countless women who embraced me and allowed me to stand in the circle. **Thank you to my Sisterhood:** Cassandra, Ebony, Shana, Kimberly, Stacia, Dalana, Tonia, Teri, Tina, Danielle, Natalie, Cheryl, Andrea "nikki", Christi, Meko, Regina, Jahnei, India, Lauren, Ivy, NaToya, Patrice, Lawanda, Ruth, Darcy, Twin, Michelle, Angelique, Freda, Tracy, Deltricia "Tawanna", Lana, Charlette, Joy "JB", Vivica, Monique, Renee, Fannie, Tekiya, Claudia, Beschelle, Paula, Jodi, Chantel, Krystal, Dionndrea " Dee Dee", Rozanda "Chilli", Shayla, Tatiana, Buffi, Pieper, Afua, Akua, Brandy, Nakeisha, Chelsea, Shanti, Sheri, Lanicia, Shyra, Toia, Bridgett, Teresa, Stacey, Sherene, Kenya, January, Holly, Alicia, Tashia, Ciera, Ebonie, Tiffany, Teia, Tunja (you are my cousin too), and the venerable Susan Taylor "You are a gem."

~~~~~~

To the fellas who had my back when I needed a little extra brawn to match my brain.

Thank you to: Ian, Mike D, Derek, Phil, Kareem, Aaron, Karl, Ozzie, Chano, Tony, KP, JNICE, Jimmy, Bryson, Myron, Big Bull, Big Mark, Big Baby, Chaka, Arbie "Lil Fate", Ludacris, Karon, Mario, Pree, JAR, Lil Jay, TLO, Che', Jason, Ryan, Ed, Lamar, Chuck, Corey, Shawn, Quincy, Jerry, Kevin "Black", Jumbo, Lil Jamez, Jamal, Drue, Dejuan, Hysaan, Eddie, Stacey, Scott, Troy, JD, Tommy, Gary "GP", My uncles of the Kappa Alpha Psi.

~~~~~~

Special thanks to Floyd Mayweather who made me the Right Hand to the Champ and gave me the priceless gifts of reflection and growth.

~~~~~~

In the stillness of very late hours in homes, in the bustle of coffee shops, in the confinement of airplanes talented and humble individuals gave of themselves and their time to give these pages a chance to find readers.

~~~~~~

My Aces

Cassandra Cousineau- My co-writer, my partner, my sister, my right side, I love you more than a pen can write and paper could hold.

Thank you Ian Burke for riding with me for over 20 years. Your belief in me and encouragement to my family has been sincerely appreciated.

~~~~~~

To My Team:

Victory is the result of the contribution of a team of individuals playing their position to perfection.

Khepra Burns-Proposal Editor Extraordinaire

Dennis Byron-Contributor to the book title

Mike DeNiro-Consultant

Lana Howard-Reader and the "*that*" police

Lynn Hinton-Reader

Kaypri-Editing support & writer of the inspiration found at dorothystory.com

Karen Lewis of Going Public PR-My publicist and woman who saw the vision before it was visible.

Kimra Major-Morris Esq and part of the original dream making team

Renae McNeil-Logo and proposal layout

John Moody-Reader

India Morel-Proposal Feedback

Ronny Myles 1badartist.com-Cover Design

Shanae Sharon-Superstar Editor

Tameka Williamson-Market Research

If there's anyone that I've forgotten please charge it to my head and not my heart.

~~~~~~

Cassandra would like thank the giver of Band-Aids, vessel of hope, and source of life her mom, Lena Morgan. Special thanks to her family, Isabelle, Braxton, and Wiley for training her in the art of existing without sleep. Especially to Philip Selvey the remarkable man who holds her heart and contributed to their loved beyond measure babies. Hugs and kisses, knuckleheads.

Many thanks and a heart full of love and respect to her sister, Tasha Robinson-White, who stands in the light and isn't afraid to lock arms with her in the darkness. This is the beginning!

Dear Reader,

Chapters that involve Tasha's job with Floyd have special lessons, something she learned as a result of being part of his environment at the end.

TABLE OF CONTENTS

PREFACE

As I began reflecting on my experiences through twelve pivotal years of my life, I found sharing my story to be therapeutic. How I defined myself became very clear. I'm a woman. I'm a mother. I'm a daughter, and because of what I've overcome, I'm a champion.

The long process of recounting these stories helped me get to know myself down to my core.

The truth is working with Floyd Mayweather was intoxicating. Having V.I.P access wasn't new to me; my entire professional career was spent around celebrities. I almost lost perspective as I got caught up in the complexity of Floyd's personality. My real friends, family, and faith were my compass, and kept me grounded.

I decided to share my story for three main reasons. First, it was important for me to reach out to other women. On my way up, I was entrenched in a patriarchal society and had to make decisions differently than a man would. I'm lucky to be part of a sisterhood that gets this. I had an untraditional job and a dream of making an impression in the world of entertainment, while fulfilling the traditional role of caring for my family.

I also wanted to set the record straight. I was often misrepresented when it came to why I no longer worked for Floyd. To some, I had a dream job. I was working for a Hall of Fame bound iconic boxer.

Finally, writing this book was therapeutic for me. I want to empower women, men, and young adults to use my story as a text book. I want people to start reading and writing again to face their fears, and overcome obstacles.

Did I tell Floyd about this book? I sure did. Not because I needed his permission, but I did get his support. In his words, "You're keeping me relevant." My intentions were not to write a book about Floyd Mayweather. This is my story, my memoir. I want to be transparent with everyone. You won't find deflections, only my journey, my life and probably your entertainment.

MY VILLAGE

I'm Tasha Robinson-White, a Midwest born and raised mother of two. Like many of you reading this story, I had goals and aspirations for my own life that I worked tirelessly to achieve. When I was hitting on all cylinders, life was euphoric. At times, I've done my fair share of crashing, and felt the burn of falling short of expectations. Through it all, I've maintained a steadfast belief that life presents itself as it should. Whether we receive our experiences as joy or pain ultimately dictates the quality of our journey. I would say unequivocally, my story of origin was the source of great joy.

I was born in Saginaw, Michigan, and eventually moved to East Lansing, while my father attended Michigan State University (MSU), home of the Spartans. Daddy was a proud member of the Kappa Alpha Psi brotherhood.

My mom and dad resembled each other so much that people mistook them for brother and sister. They were both butterscotch-complexioned with thick, wavy, brown hair. Black and white photographs taken during the years they were dating flaunted their 1970s "sho-nuff" inspired afros. Mom and dad's birthdays were four days apart in the last week of March, on the 22nd and 26th respectively. They had trademark fiery Aries personalities.

My dad's piercing green, hazel-eyes, were likely a calling card with the ladies in his younger days. "Big L" was a stocky wrestler in high-school. My dad stood 5'8" tall, but to me he was seven feet on the inside. He was a forthright man who was known for finishing his sentences with an affirmative nod, "You understand." Anyone who sat down to challenge him to a chess-match heard daddy's interpretation of life and that phrase incessantly.

My mom affectionately went by Bea, short for Willabea. At 5'7", her lanky frame floated into the room. Her doe-like, almond brown eyes were passed on to my brothers and me. They made her "don't test me, child" glare even more potent. My close friends called her Miss Bea as she couldn't stand to be called Mama Bea. To refer to my mom as a spirited woman would be an understatement. Mom could size up a situation and bluntly give her opinion without much deliberation. She was a quick witted, smart, woman of substance. I could easily say that my mom was the woman I wanted to grow up to become.

Depending on the day, and angle you were standing at, you could say I looked a little like the both of them, with the exception of my height. Well, lack thereof. The measuring stick stopped when I hit 5'1" and a half (yes, I hold on to that half). It helped that I inherited my mom's sense of humor.

We lived in an MSU community called Spartan Village, while a young Earvin "Magic" Johnson was ballin' hard for the University. He was a neighbor, and at the time I was only tangentially aware of his Hall of Fame skills. To me, he was a tall brother with an infectious smile, who played basketball.

Spartan Village was a unique place -- an environment that changed in language, culture and culinary scents every other block. I grew up with Muslims, Christians and Buddhists as friends. It felt like utopia.

As a young person, I learned how to make $1.00 out of 59 cents. So did many of my childhood friends. My Spartan Village crew including the Austin siblings

Alexis, Dane and Ravonia, washed windows and swept patios around the neighborhood with me to earn spending money.

I was destined for a career in entertainment. It was evident before I was out of elementary school, as I was bitten by the performing bug early. Spartan Village had an annual spring festival called *The Rites of Spring*. It was a carnival complete with games, fried food, and entertainment.

My introduction to the spotlight came at age six, during a contest featured at one of those festivals. There was a performance pavilion with a small stage and corded microphone. That mic stand was like a magnet that drew me towards it without even thinking. I made a spontaneous decision to sing for the small crowd gathered in front of the portable stairs. I dragged my bubbly, down for anything girlfriend, Nikki Stewart, on stage with me too. Nikki jumped up forgetting that she had a soft pink roller still setting a bang in her hair.

I sang a song that had special meaning to my family at the time. My mom and I had been living in Oberlin, Ohio, while my dad was getting situated at

MSU. It was only fitting that I sang *Reunited* by Peaches and Herb.

I swayed back and forth with the mic in my hand giving each note equal emphasis. In my mind I was competing on *Star Search,* a similar show to *American Idol.* I sang my heart out and won! Part of the prize was an invitation to perform and be interviewed on the University's television station.

Public speaking came easily to me. I didn't spend too much time prepping for the interview. I poured all of my energy into my performance. I just knew it was my big break and I had the perfect song in mind. *Rock with You* by Michael Jackson gave me a chance to show off some of my dancing moves.

I went all out by practicing in the two-toned, brown, and gray rabbit fur coat my godmother Marg sent me from Lansing. I strutted in my coat like I was Tracey Quartermaine, my favorite character on *General Hospital.* I reenacted her lines around the house all of the time. I credit my mother with introducing me to soaps, which we called *"the stories"* back then.

After the show aired I thought I made it to the big time. I was going to be a child star for sure. As often as I could, I auditioned and participated in plays and shows in my community. If you asked me today if I can sing I will say, "No, but I sure can act like I can with confidence."

I was an only child for eight years until my brother Lawrence "Low" was born. Kahil came a year and half later. You could easily tell we were siblings by looking at us. My brothers were super-cute kids who grew-up to be handsome men. Occasionally, a classmate would ask if they were bi-racial, or Asian because of the texture of their hair and deep almond eyes. Low was just over six feet and had the same butterscotch complexion as my parents and I. Kahil, the baby, was slightly darker and maybe an inch or so shorter than Low. I must have left a few extra inches for them in my mom's womb.

I matured quickly by having two younger brothers around while my parents were still young themselves. I spent my early teens babysitting them while Mom and Dad partied. Babysitting never really bothered me except when I wanted to go somewhere and couldn't. Our alone time without our parents made my brothers and I very close. As kids, we weren't aware that the bond we were creating was unbreakable.

We didn't have any sibling rivalry; we were a tight-knit family. We covered for each other so that none of us would get in trouble by our parents. One time in particular, I stole my parent's car to take them to play in the park. I took the responsibility my parent's entrusted in me seriously though. I wouldn't let my brothers have company when we were home alone. It was a give and take relationship.

We were harmless and kept our parent's voice in the back of our heads. Mom and Dad would repeatedly say, "Never lie to us. Never steal from us." These were simple foundation building instructions that we respected.

My father encouraged me tell him the truth even when it was bad news. Daddy let it be known that he and my mother would always be able to handle whatever we had done. I tested this when I hit a boy with a baseball bat. I was defending my little brother Low after the boy called him a Nigger. I came home crying and managed to tell him the story through my hyperventilating sniffles. I was scared my father would be arrested because I thought I gave the boy a concussion. My dad remained composed and even told me to go back outside to play.

My parents had experienced real racial discrimination and hardship. That word wasn't just a word, it was a symbol of oppression that we had zero tolerance for. Daddy understood my indignation when defending my brother. They didn't condone violence in our house, but mom and dad didn't believe in us backing down from anyone.

Nothing ever came of the baseball bat incident. That taught me that when people know they're wrong, they either get extra loud to deflect attention elsewhere, or they act like nothing ever happened. That boy chose the latter, and I know he walked lightly whenever I came around. I heard he told someone that I was crazy.

I kept in touch with my classmates and "play cousins" even as I changed school districts. Back in the day, "play cousins" were friends we weren't related to, but still considered family. Teri Porter became my play cousin when I first moved to Spartan Village. I was thankful to already know someone at my new school, when I transferred from East Lansing to Sexton High my freshman year.

Teri encouraged me to audition for the school talent show with her and two other girls, Fyquetia

Scates and Tracey Alexander. These girls were a year or two older than us, but they were Elegante's; a junior sorority mentored by the Alpha Kappa Alpha, "AKA" sorority. Eventually, Tracy would become my big sister and Fyquetia became Teri's.

We acted so grown trying to sing *Sexy* by Klymaxx. My mom wouldn't really let me wear make-up as a freshman in high school. She bent the rules for the talent show. She also gave me the freedom to choose my own outfit to perform in. We wore tight denim bottoms with black and white laced negligées. I even straightened my long, wispy, hair down which I didn't do very often back then. That talent show was epic. It set the stage for many performances throughout my high school years.

I was surrounded by talented singers, dancers, rappers and actors. J Rock was a local rapper/singer who went to another school. He was kind of like the Drake of our time. My friends John Poww and his brother Shawn formed a group called UNV. We were so proud of them when their single, *Something's Going On,* was released in 1993, by Madonna's label Maverick Records.

I can't talk about Sexton talent shows without mentioning Craig "Coops" Cooper, and Eddie and Richard Robinson. They had pipes and lived on my block on Wainwright. They were like younger versions of R&B legends Luther Vandross and Gerald Levert. I can still envision their dance steps and recount every note those boys sang.

I eventually became an Elegante' and threw myself into event planning and step shows. I was probably the last one to get the choreography down, but I did it! After I was elected as the Secretary, I borrowed a name from one of my Daddy's Funkadelic albums for pledges to address me. I was "T-Live is Supergroovealasticprofunkstacation the lovely secretary with all the information." They had to mimic the neck roll that I did too.

My parents knew the importance of being part of a community. Now that I think about it, my parents were awesome. They opened their home to a lot of people, especially my friends whose parents commuted from city to city for work during the weekdays. Everyone knew the rules. If one of my friends got out of line, my parents' circle of friends had an agreement to extend discipline to each other's homes.

My friends Buffi and Pieper Green stayed with us for a short time. They grew quite fond of my parents, nicknaming them George and Weezy after the characters from the television show *The Jeffersons.*

Tatiana "Tanya" Maliwe from Spartan Village ended up living with us her senior year of high school. She was two years older than me. Most of my friends were two to four years my senior. I was mature for my age and ended up attracting the attention of older boys as a result of my demeanor. My first boyfriend, Forrest, and I met at the mall when I was 13. I was in middle school, and he was a senior in high school. So, I lied and told him I was 14, going on 15, and in the ninth grade. Since we went to separate schools, we phone dated for a few months.

I hosted gatherings at my house which we called "sets". My first "set", was actually my 14th birthday party. I invited Forrest and his friends to come by. I didn't immediately think about my age being exposed. A few older friends were going to attend and Forrest should have felt right at home.

My parents were always home during the sets. They trusted me and mostly left us alone during the night. Everything was cool until it was time sing *Happy Birthday*. My mom brought out my favorite chocolate cake with white cream cheese icing, she lit 14 candles, and I was busted.

Forrest was surprised I was only 14, but didn't want to break-up with me because of my age. Our moms felt differently. When Forrest invited me over to meet his parents his mom confronted me. "I know you're not 16, you're too young to be dating an 18 year-old," she issued a stern warning. His mom was not playing with me.

The next day, she made Forrest call my house to tell my parents that we had been dating. I kept hanging up on him when he called, trying to avoid being put on punishment by my mom. When he finally got her on the phone, that's exactly what happened. I was forbidden from seeing him ever again. She threatened Forrest too. "You don't know Tasha. Forget her number. Stay away from my house!"

Even though our families didn't approve, we continued to sneak around trying to see each other. We were eventually caught by my Uncle Thomas when he saw Forrest dropping me off near my house while my dad was at work. Uncle Thomas made us both go inside to have a heart-to-heart. That talk didn't go so well. All I remember was him being chased down our block on Bessemaur by our German Shepard. I screamed, "Run, Forrest, Run!" Our relationship ended when Forrest entered the Army after he graduated.

My friends teased me because they used to say I stayed on punishment. Now, as a mother I know that my parents were protecting me from being a minor who made major mistakes.

My family traveled a lot when I was growing up. We were part of a caravan of family members that drove from Chicago to Mississippi every summer. Around the Fourth of July, family from Saginaw and Flint collected us in Lansing, and we all continued on to Chicago. We spent the night there, picked up more family, and traveled to Eupora, Mississippi, to visit my great grandparents. By the time we reached them, we were a caravan of about forty to fifty kids and adults.

Most of the men in my family who lived in Michigan, worked at the Oldsmobile plants located in Bay City and Flint. We had a wide-bodied, four door, burgundy Buick Regal. When I sat in the passenger's seat, I couldn't see the road over the "Property of the Robinson's" custom plate stuck to the dashboard. Daddy kept his car spick and span. It was washed down and smelled new in the beginning, middle, and end of every excursion.

As each car joined the trip, drivers plugged in CBs that were like walkie-talkies in your car. Everybody introduced themselves using their unique handle. My grandfather was, "Big E" while my dad was, "The Mothership Connection." *Mutha Ship* as he would pronounce it. In case you don't know, *The Mothership Connection* was the fourth album by the funk band, Parliament and the Funkadelics.

I wasn't a driver, but my dad called me, "The Grasshopper." To him, I was like the curious, patient, young guy in the T.V. show Kung Fu. The wise old man in the beginning of the show said, "If you can take the pebble from my hand it will be time for you to leave." That phrase became an inside joke between daddy and me. He switched out the word pebble for quarter.

When he signed off from driving he kiddingly said, "The Mutha Ship is about to let The Grasshopper take over as driver." I learned to drive at the age of eleven during one of those trips.

Europa was a small town where my great grandfather, Daddy Frank, raised hogs and horses. The population is still barely over 2,000 residents today. When we reached city limits the whole town knew we were there. It wasn't uncommon to be asked at the local market, "Which Robinson are you?"

My father used our trips to expose us to our heritage and family history. We visited the Robinson Cemetery and learned about the lives of our relatives who had long been buried in those grounds. Both my grandmother and Papa were Robinson's before they were married. I was probably related to most of the people in Europa.

We ended many of our days sitting out in the yard with a fire burning in a big ole pot, swatting mosquitoes, and sharing stories.

My parents made sure we had relationships with members on both sides of our family. At least once a year we visited my mom's relatives in Cleveland and Oberlin, Ohio. Staying with Grandma Flossie and Papa Croft allowed me to satisfy two of my childhood fascinations; riding rollercoasters at Cedar Point, and catching frogs in the backyard.

I loved toads as a kid. They seemed to be everywhere when we went to Ohio. I was admonished over and over again not to bring any frogs into the house. I couldn't help myself. I was obsessed with them. I liked the peculiar way their bumpy skin felt. So as not to get in trouble, I hid one in a box on the family's front porch. To me, that wasn't the house, it was technically an extension of the outside. The toad hopped out of the box and gave Papa Croft a heart attack. I never brought one inside or near the house again.

My dad had four younger sisters, Joyce, Yvonne, Cathy, and Beverly. All of them were involved in my upbringing, but I was closer to Beverly and Cathy. They were only ten years older than me. I idolized and wanted to be like them as if they were my big sisters. When I visited my grandparents, I couldn't wait for them to get dressed to go out for the night. I sat in the bedroom with them and picked out clothes as if I was in my aunties' pretend store.

Cathy and Beverly were my babysitters when I visited Saginaw, and once they got married and had kids, I returned the favor by watching my cousins.

Being exposed to individuals from all walks of life has helped me get along with and respect people from diverse backgrounds. I benefited from a rock-solid support system in that I've never been intimidated to change, or try something different. I would always be grounded in the Midwest. My family and all that I had grown to love were there.

FOUND LOVE IN COLLIPARK

It's been my experience that God hasn't tapped me on the shoulder and whispered, "This is a life changing event." Usually, I have a plan and then "the plan" is revealed. Immediately after graduating high school in 1990, my plan was to move to Atlanta and pursue a degree in Mass Communications from Spelman, an all-women's HBCU.

I moved to Atlanta for a fresh start. The city was becoming ground zero for the Black entrepreneurial revolution. In particular, the music industry there was introducing new sounds and artists making it the Motown of the South. Though I wasn't necessarily seeking to be a performer anymore, I still wanted to be around entertainment. The opportunities and people of this city grew on me fast.

I stayed with my Aunt Beverly and her boyfriend Aaron until school started. They both helped me get acclimated to "The Peach State." Aaron came from a family of nine. He had four brothers and four sisters.

His middle brother, Kevin, was a dancer and close to my age. Aaron and Beverly asked Kevin to introduce me to a few people and show me around the city.

When I found out Kevin was a dancer, I jumped at the chance to tell him that I was an Elegante'. He and his homeboy Paul challenged me to a battle. I was all bravado about how I could hang. They thought I was real competition until I conceded minutes into the battle. They were yekin and everything. Yekin started off in the skating rinks in the South. When somebody pulled off a hot move they stomped really hard and threw their hands up like, "Yeah, I did that." I loved my Aunt Beverly, but it was fun to spend time with people my own age.

Kevin called me in the evening after our dance off, I presumed to gloat some more. His sense of humor matched mine, and even though he had swag, his Southern charm reminded me of the Midwest men that I grew up around. I admired his intelligence and sense of fairness. We could talk about anything.

The conversation moved on to holiday plans since the next day was the Fourth of July. I was supposed to go to Six Flags with a guy I recently met. He seemed nice and friendly until our conversations started to get more sexual. I wasn't ready for that with him at the time.

Kevin was taking his girlfriend to Six Flags as well. It was thoughtful of him to offer be my wing man if my date went awry. I remember hanging up the phone thinking that I had a brother in Atlanta. We were definitely going to be good friends.

I was getting ready for bed when my Six Flags date called to talk about sex again. After my conversation with Kevin, I was so bored with this guy. I told him it wasn't going down like that. He was one of those guys who insisted that he could "change my mind" once I saw him again.

I still wanted to go to the park and he was my ride. I played it cool knowing that Kevin was my backup plan. The next morning, I was hyped to ride the roller coasters and see the fireworks display at the end of the day. I looked fly in my saggy, purple, MC Hammer pants. I wore them with a black, midriff bearing, off the shoulder shirt. I pulled back my long hair with a matching headband and waited. I waited, and waited. By 1:00 that afternoon it was clear that my date was a no show. He "changed my mind" alright.

Thankfully, Kevin called to check on me. "Are you still going to Six Flags?" he asked in that same brotherly voice that I heard the night before. I told him that I wanted to go, but I think the guy got the hint that I wasn't going to have sex with him, and he low key dissed me.

For whatever reason, Kevin and his girlfriend had an argument. She cancelled on him, but he still wanted to go. His father had given him $100 and he wanted me to help him spend it. I didn't think we were on a date until Kevin started putting his arm around me as if I was his girl. We even took a picture with him holding me by the waist at one of those photo stands. He gave me the picture on our way out of the park. He probably couldn't keep it at his house for his girlfriend to see.

Kevin already told me he didn't really like riding roller coaster. He especially didn't like the ones with a steep drop. I did, so I dragged him to all of those rides. By the time the fireworks started, we were holding hands. It seemed natural because we spent the whole day together at the park. My hand fit in his and his fit in mine.

Kevin was so cute with his high right, low left, Kid and Play haircut. His smooth chocolate complexion made his perfect white teeth stand out even more. I was always into a nice smile even though I had a crooked smile with a gap between my two front teeth. He was slender, but I could feel how fit he was through his shirt when we hugged goodbye.

In the days that followed, we didn't have a conversation about our date at Six Flags. He remained in his relationship while we matter-of-factly went about our friendship as if nothing happened. For many months, I denied my feelings for Kevin because I hadn't gone to Atlanta to start a relationship.

I felt homesick during the holiday season. I wanted to spend time with my little brothers and the rest of my family in Michigan. I wasn't able to travel because of my work schedule. I hadn't built up any vacation time with the retail job I was working in Atlanta.

I tried to pretend that I was going about my business and being responsible, but Kevin sensed sadness in the tone of my voice on Thanksgiving Day. He offered to take me to the Macy's Christmas tree lighting ceremony in downtown Atlanta. Macy's knows how to put on a holiday show. It was a picturesque scene of lights, music, and magically festive. That huge tree made downtown Atlanta smell like Christmas.

As we walked arm-in-arm through the illustrious display, I was lost in Kevin's stories as he shared more about who he was. When he disclosed that he was unhappy with his girlfriend. I thought, *here we go; he's planting a seed to see if I am interested*.

I was giving Kevin an earful about starting my life in Atlanta when he cut me off mid-sentence with the touch of his lips on mine. No boy had ever kissed me like that in all of my eighteen years. He kissed me like a man would kiss a woman. It took me a couple of seconds to pull away. "You still have a girlfriend," I asserted while wiping my lips. He called her immediately and ended their relationship. I was sympathetic for her and flattered for me at the same time.

Since he was a free man, I wanted to go back to that kiss. The tree lighting event closed down and neither of us was ready to call it a night. I hesitated for half a second when he invited me back to his parent's house. We quietly entered the home trying to go unnoticed by his younger siblings Patrice, Lawanda, and baby brother Chalonzo who were also living there.

Kevin's bedroom was located in the basement of the family's house. It was quiet and secluded from the rest of the rooms. We went undetected. Kevin's selection of background music, the *Quiet Storm on KISS 104.1FM*, was all the atmosphere needed to keep up kissing and cuddling for hours.

I would have slept in that morning if it wasn't for his mother's gentle knock at the door. "Kevin, are you still taking me to work?" We both jumped up still fully clothed. I was embarrassed that this was my first introduction to his mother. He even played it off by mumbling something about me being Beverly's niece. That was the best he could do since the last she knew he had a girlfriend, and I wasn't her.

Kevin and I became inseparable. They say that a girl seeks a man who reminds her of her father, especially when it comes to matters of the heart. Kevin and my dad were both romantic men. Daddy used to sing *Superstar* by Luther Vandross to my mom, and Kevin also had a beautiful singing voice. He was my renaissance man who could do just about anything. I never would've guessed that he was a fisherman. We spent time on Lake Lanier on the outskirts of Atlanta. We found secluded areas for him to catch bass, and catfish, while I sun bathed nude on nearby rocks.

Watching how he interacted with his family, especially his mother, made me fall in love with him. Family was important to me, and I wanted to be with a man who shared those values.

Kevin and his siblings had a team mentality that came from the days of their youth. They were encouraged by their father to excel at athletics. The family set school records in seven different sports while attending North Clayton High School, in College Park, just outside of Atlanta. They participated in everything from track and field to baseball and wrestling. Hard work contributed to their success and they were definitely genetically gifted.

When his older brother Karl was drafted as a slot receiver by the Atlanta Falcons, the whole family celebrated. Karl shared his success by helping Kevin and Aaron open a teen nightclub on Old National Highway. The two of them had been hosting parties in apartment club houses off Godby Road. The club made them official promoters.

A lot of up-and-coming Atlanta based celebrities showed up at the club Tru Flava. The Boys, Xscape (back then they went by Precise), Another Bad Creation (ABC), Kris Kross, TLC, Eddie Weathers and Jermaine Dupri of So So Def, Da Brat, Jena Se Qua, Lil Malley G, and even Ludacris. This was way before he was Luda; back then he went by Chris. Rasheeda came through with Kia and Keke from her group the Kartoon Kapers. Our boy Troy was on the turntables, and our friends Stacy, Scott and Chuck were in charge of marketing and promotions. We were a hit!

Cutting my teeth in the early Atlanta music scene prepared me to grind until I got results. My neighbor and good friend Chelsea Gray, who worked at LaFace, knew of an opening at the label. I was working with the venerable Ian Burke, as an assistant with Greenhouse Management, while he managed Xscape. He previously managed TLC.

Ian's reputation in the industry added credibility to Chelsea's recommendation to Davette Singletary. She ran the Artists Development department, but was known as the Mama of LaFace. Seriously, nobody made a major decision until Davette signed off.

She brought me on as an intern and made a commitment to find a way to hire me as an employee. "If there is a will there is a way," she assured me. I had the will and Davette made a way to get me that check.

She was impressed with the rapport I built with the staff and most of the artists. I interacted with every department at the label; Product Management, Publicity, Marketing and Promotions, and even Video Production with Director Billie Woodruff.

I chose to withdraw from Spelman. My education was gained in the workforce through working alongside smart, business savvy woman including Shanti Das (Author of *Hip Hop Professionals*), Chelsea Patterson (Superstar wife and mother of two) and Sheri Riley (Founder and CEO of Glue Incorporated).

Davette was a one of a kind mentor. She gave me access to her industry Rolodex to manually enter it into a spreadsheet. She told me to make a copy for myself after I was finished. I was reluctant to take her up on her offer at first. A colleague at LaFace was astonished that Davette trusted me so much. Even then, I only copied some of the contacts. I wasn't going to be able to call Michael Jackson without a formal introduction anyway.

I contributed to the grass roots marketing campaign for Usher's self-titled debut album. One of my most exciting projects was the mega album release party for Outkast, the Southernplayalisticadillacmuzik picnic. Most artists that were signed under the Arista umbrella performed there. I got to see Biggie and Craig Mac in their first Atlanta performance. I gained a lot of marketing and promotions ideas from that event.

After Davette passed away in 2011, I realized that I gained something far greater than a book of contacts. Davette, Shanti, Sheri, and Chelsea were the original members of my career sisterhood. I have an enormous amount of respect for those who work behind the scenes of some of today's most recognizable celebrities. To me, the work that goes on off camera makes what you see on camera possible.

While I was working at LaFace, Kevin was managing a group of five pre-teenage boys from the Godby Road area named the Owd Squad. Their singing, rapping and dancing was similar to the group ABC that was discovered by Michael Bivens. Kevin was a great mentor to those boys. He had a special touch when it came to motivating young people. Maybe he benefitted from needing to compromise a lot with his many brothers and sisters. He paid attention when the boys in the group expressed their opinions, and treated them each as individuals. The man had the gift of patience.

I would have to write another book to describe what I witnessed driving in the Godby Road section of town. One day in particular, when Kevin and I arrived to pick up the boys for rehearsal, they were all standing on one side of the street while two older guys stared hard at them on the opposite corner. When Kevin got out of the car, the Owd Squad told him they were being threatened by a guy named Bae Bae. The boys were 11 and 12 while Bae Bae was our age. His beef with them was nothing but jealousy. He was trying to punk them and Kevin was having none of it.

I stayed in the car until I heard Bae Bae getting louder and louder. When I got across the street, Kevin had Bae Bae in some sort of wrestling lock. I was Kevin's back up no matter what the situation turned out to be. I kicked Bae Bae in the head with my steel toe Doc Martins and dared his little homie to jump in. I was ready to fight a dude that day. Kevin had to grab my leg, while he was fighting, and scream, "Bay (our pet name for one another), chill I got this."

I felt like I needed to protect Kevin and the Owd Squad. They were really like our kids. We got them out of the hood as much as possible. They mostly came from single parent households, and their mothers were grateful when we let the boys stay over at my apartment a few days a week. We gave them clothes when they had a performance, drove them around in my car, and made sure they ate a decent meal. I was the unofficial team Mom.

The Godby Road incident wasn't the only time I was in a fist fight around Kevin. A few years later, I was celebrating New Year's Day at the club 112 with my girls Kim, Chelsea, and Shana. We met up with Kevin and his friends at another club named The Warehouse. I had been drinking and by the time midnight rolled around I was drunk. When I got to the Warehouse, the first thing I saw was my man at the stage with a girl kneeling down in front of him. It looked like she was trying to do something sexual to him. I saw red and all of the colors in the rainbow. I jumped over Kevin and punched the girl dead in her face. No questions asked.

Kevin had to throw me over his shoulder while I was kicking and screaming out of the club. Once we were outside, he told me that the woman I punched was his homeboy's girlfriend. She was inviting us to a house party. He took me back inside to apologize.

In 1994, after four years of dating, he proposed to me during a trip to Cancun. I was hopeful that he had sowed all of his wild oats and was ready to settle down for real. I was still showing off my 24 karat gold, one carat clustered engagement ring when our relationship came off the rails. I was miffed from getting wind of his indiscretions and disrespectful conduct. We were young and living in a city where Kevin had a past. He was still known as an entertainer in Atlanta, and enjoyed the attention from local women a bit too much.

I decided to separate from him and move to Las Vegas to be with my family who had relocated there. Kevin had to outgrow the need to "kick it" and become fully committed to settling down with one woman. Kevin didn't want me to leave. He promised to change his ways. I didn't believe he could while we lived in Atlanta.

As the plane taxied down the runway my eyes burned, and were partially swollen from a night's worth of tears. Nothing felt right about me leaving. I believed if Kevin's heart was truly mine, and mine his, we would make our way back to each other. When I landed in Vegas, my father was there to greet me and wipe my tears away. I already missed Kevin so much.

It took him about two months to join me. Ironically, our love reconnected and grew in the desert. Kevin came on Memorial Day weekend for what was supposed to be a two day vacation. He ended up staying for a lifetime. We found out I was pregnant with our daughter Jaelin.

My parents didn't mind letting Kevin live with us, even though they were adamant that we couldn't share a bed until we were husband and wife. He was employed as a maintenance worker and contributed as much as he could. Kevin had always been a talented craftsman. He was capable of building an entire house from the ground up, including installation of air conditioning, and plumbing.

On August 5, 1995, we took my little brothers to Circus Circus Casino to celebrate Kahil's birthday. While the boys were riding the roller coasters Kevin urged me to make it official. "Let's get married today. Let's just do it." I was elated and proudly consented to be his wife. We pulled up to the drive-through of The Little White Chapel on Las Vegas Boulevard. Kahil and Low were our witnesses from the back of the car.

We went back to Atlanta to celebrate Thanksgiving that year. While we were there, Kevin's friend and well-known choreographer, Devyne Stephens, got him an audition as a back-up dancer with Monica right before she was headed out for her first tour. We both ended up extending our Atlanta trip to pursue creative endeavors.

On a whim, I auditioned for a local gospel play, "A Change Is Gonna Come" I found in the back pages of Creative Loafing magazine. Days before I was supposed to head back to Vegas, the Director, Lisa Wu (Lisa Wu Sweat at the time), called and offered me the leading role of Tish. I had to rush home and make it back to Atlanta before rehearsal kicked off on December 30.

An unknown was Lisa's assistant Director. He was really intense when he came to set. So was the theme of the play that also featured actor Todd Bridges. I was one half of an interracial couple that experienced a series of hardships. I remember the assistant Director giving me notes to "work the stage" and "use my space." I didn't know who he was, nor could I have ever guessed how successful Tyler Perry would become.

After the Monica tour, Kevin was booked as a dancer on the TLC tour. He stayed on the road for the better part of two years. Friends and family constantly told him he was lucky to have a girl like me to support his creative dreams. I thought we were lucky to have each other.

HUSTLE IS MY DNA

I have a history of juggling a handful of projects at one time. I always had a hustle. As a child, I told my mom that I would have a nice house, with a cleaning staff, fly on private jets, and have a closet full of stylish shoes. I found a way to make most of that happen through how I structured my career.

After high school, I had at least a dozen different jobs to pay my bills. I worked as a leasing agent and apartment complex manager. I even spent time working at a mental hospital. More than being busy, I liked to be productive.

My hustle was the impetus that led to the job that would change my life forever. It started out in the uncharacteristically chilly Las Vegas winter of 1997. I was promoting a Billboard Music Awards after party at Club Utopia on the Las Vegas Strip. I cold called the owner David Cohen to see if he'd let me rent out the spot.

I've managed to look a few years younger than my actual age for most of my life. Undoubtedly, my mouth full of braces made me appear less seasoned than I was. When I met with David, I was this fresh faced kid with long, dark brown, tightly straw-set curly hair. I learned that style from my girl Shana in Atlanta. The skill allowed me to make a fair amount of side money charging $70 a head when I moved to Las Vegas. My clients grabbed a generous amount of straws from McDonalds, or Burger King and I created ribbons of curls dancing around the nape and crown of their heads.

With the confidence of a promoter twice my senior, I laid out my plan for the promotion. David was a long blond haired hipster type who was open to trying something different at his club. He listened to my pitch, but needed to be convinced I was capable of competing with promoters who had a track record in the area. He would only consider me if I put up $4,000. Half of which, he needed right away. I had heard that the rental fee was actually $2,000. I agreed to the inflated price to capitalize on the opportunity.

Initially, I had a hard time confirming artists. In order to get the marketing material printed in time I had to use the old "special invited guest" tactic. I pounded the pavement with fliers and, purchased a few promotional radio spots to drive local interest. I prayed my calls to labels and managers would result in a few big names showing up.

Most people don't realize it, but at events like this celebrities are paid to come to a venue. These are called walk-throughs. Back in the day they showed up on the strength of relationships. Celebrities, mostly their managers, changed the game by inventing the walk-through pay in the early 2000s. This created opportunities to make appearance money without committing to an entire night.

My efforts paid off. The party was packed with celebrities representing every genre of music from country super star Garth Brooks, to Usher and hip hop pioneer Queen Latifah. I had to turn Leanne Rimes away because she was under age. My girl Alicia introduced me to Simp, our DJ for the night. He brought along local deejays Warren Peace and Mr. Bob from KLUC 98.5. Coincidentally, I used to send the two of them vinyl during my days at LaFace.

Somewhere between playing Puffy's *Been around the World* and Bone Thugs and Harmony, who also happened to be in the club when Simp called me to the booth. A man named Jeff wanted to bring his nephew into the party, but he was under age. Simp pleaded with me, "Floyd Mayweather is a boxer and doesn't drink. He won't be any trouble."

"Floyd Mary what?" I asked, mispronouncing his last name the first time I heard it. He shouted, "Floyd Mayweather! Tasha he's going to be one of the best boxers in the world and you need to know him."

I wasn't trying to mess up my relationship with David Cohen so some kid could come into the club. I only went to meet Jeff's nephew at the door to see if I had to turn him away.

Floyd embodied every sense of his boxing moniker "Pretty Boy." He was impeccably groomed from head to toe. His low cut fade showed off a perfect pattern of waves created by sleeping in a wave cap to lay his hair down. His rich, brown, skin was unblemished and smooth like a newborn. He was a good looking young guy.

Thirty degrees isn't the same cold that I grew up with in the Midwest, but it was cold enough for Floyd to wear a fur coat to the club that night. He was decked out in the brightest, matching, Coogie clothes from head to toe. He set his whole outfit off in shined up royal blue alligator shoes. He looked like a young boy playing dress-up in his father's best macking clothes.

David was already out there. He knew Floyd and co-signed to let him in. I didn't have much to say. I was working and looked passed this teenager trying to crash my party.

The next time I saw Floyd was in late January of 1998, at another party where Simp was spinning. He was at a club near the UNLV campus called The Wet Stop for reggae night. My girlfriend Christi came in from Atlanta to celebrate my 26th birthday. My crew Ebony, Alicia, Drina and Melissa joined us at the club.

Simp came out of the booth to formally introduce me to Floyd and his best friend Shaun Tyler who he called Head. Shaun must've had a fake ID since he was still in high school at the time.

They were flossing with gators on again. They looked like two grown ass men. When I extended my hand to Floyd, he gripped it firmly and held it a little too long. He asked, "When can I take you to dinner?" I laughed and replied, "You can't, I'm married." "No problem," he back peddled. "When can I take you and your husband to dinner? We need to discuss how you know all these celebrities." I was not about to ask Kevin to come to dinner with me and another man, but Floyd was persistent. He was impressed by my Billboard party and thought we could team up to promote more events in Las Vegas.

I let him talk while he was buying us drinks. I thought he was just some guy trying to impress a group of women by spending money on them.

He stuck around all night. When we walked out, he made it a point to let me know he was driving the brand new blue Lexus out there. I guess that was really supposed to impress me. I smirked, "Yeah, you're parked next to my red convertible Mustang." We went our separate ways without exchanging contact information.

A day later, Kevin, Christi and I went to club Utopia to continue celebrating my birthday. Floyd and his crew were there again. Believe it or not, he wasn't on the scene too frequently in his early boxing days, especially not while he was in training camp. Neither of us was. It just so happened that we ran into each other a lot during a short period of time. I would come to learn that he was more humble than his choice in clothing made him appear.

I already mentioned to Kevin that Floyd expressed interest in future promotions when we spoke at the Wet Stop. He had already gotten the rundown from me when Floyd approached us in front of Utopia. At first, Floyd didn't notice Kevin standing next to me when he reached out to shake my hand. I shifted a little to get the two of them face to face for an introduction.

I was enjoying myself until a woman gave Kevin a hug from behind while we were dancing. I was embarrassed when I caught a glimpse of Floyd smirking as he was looking at us. I really feel that was the first sign of weakness Floyd sensed in my relationship. I was seething inside and couldn't show it. If I made it an issue, I would look weak in front of Floyd and Christi. So, I kept my mouth shut.

A pattern developed around how I would run into Floyd. Every time I saw Simp, Floyd was there too. Two months later, Simp told me to stop by his house and pick up some mixed CD's he wanted me to listen to. He enjoyed passing out music for people to hear new artists. I already had plans to go out that night to show off my new short haircut. Over the years, I became known for changing up the cut, color, and style of my hair quite regularly. I've sported a blond pixie, a cropped highlighted bob, and a little of everything in between.

When I got to his house, Simp felt the need to re-introduce us as if I forgot who Floyd was. For his part, Floyd was full of compliments each time we crossed paths. I never felt like he was coming on to me. His boyish charm was endearing and made him extraordinarily likeable.

I had to pick up Ebony in Summerlin, not far from Floyd's house. He offered to escort me out there. Not like I needed a ride along, but I could tell he was coming whether I asked him or not. I didn't mind his company. I was intrigued by him.

When we really got to talking we were like two old friends that had to catch up on the last ten years of our lives. We even discovered that we were both from the same home state! He grew up in Grand Rapids, forty-five minutes from Lansing.

He and his friend ended up connecting with me and Ebony later that night. We finally exchanged contact information. I gave him my pager (yes we used pagers back then) number and he passed along his cell number. We spent a few hours driving up and down the Las Vegas strip on that windy February evening. I was having so much fun talking about the plans we had for ourselves, I paid no attention to the cold weather.

I felt like we were in our own movie. We flashed by the hotel marquis and all we needed was a soundtrack playing in the background. For a young guy he thought really big, way beyond throwing parties with celebrities. He had plans to conquer the boxing world and become a successful entrepreneur.

By this time, Jaelin was barely two years old and I was a mom and a wife. Floyd on the other hand wanted a lot of children. He conveyed, "Tasha I want what you have." When he shared that, he made me feel really uncomfortable. I didn't know what he meant. When he started talking about his kids I figured it out. He wanted someone to be down for him unconditionally like what I shared with Kevin. His girlfriend, Melissia, had a baby boy from a previous relationship. I could tell he really loved the both of them.

He explained that when he did have kids of his own, he wanted to live alone in his mansion, and for the kids to live with their mom in another. I couldn't process that. It's actually how it went down though. His four children have always lived with their mothers in separate homes he has provided. This was his version of a family.

Floyd grew up as the only son of four children. He had three sisters. Floyd and Fatima had the same father. While him and his sisters Fannie, and Tawanna had the same mother. He initially told me Tawanna was his twin sister. Once I met Tawanna, she told me he told a lot of people that. He was good for dropping little white lies.

Maybe they weren't twins, but Floyd and his siblings all had beautiful, flawless brown skin, especially Fannie. Her chiseled, strong facial features made her a unique beauty. If she were a few inches taller, Floyd's baby sister would easily have been a fashion model.

We went our separate ways after our talk and didn't cross paths in clubs too much after that. I was doing me and he was doing him. Vegas was, and still is, a town full of people on their grind. It was as if you could drive in, find a place to stay, and a job all in the same day. Infamously known for its back-room deals, the city was also the epicenter of instant opportunities. I was made for a town like this.

I took advantage of the luminescent Strip to find ways to create income for myself. In addition to promoting clubs, I was working at Hilton Grand Vacation Club as a tour coordinator, and was hired to dress as a Roman princess, greeting guests at Caesars Palace Casino. I maintained my music industry connections by booking talent to sing the national anthem for a short-lived Vegas based basketball team. Floyd stopped by rehearsals from time to time to bend my ear about starting his record label, Philthy Rich.

I heard more about him as months passed. With Las Vegas being a boxing Mecca, a lot of people began to notice this charismatic, rising star. I finally realized he was a serious boxer with real potential. He wouldn't have to pull strings to get into the next event Kevin and I were planning.

Kevin, his brother Aaron and I were promoting a concert with Bad Boy artist, 112, in the spring of 1999. The venue wanted extra security because there was uneasiness surrounding the West Coast, East Coast rivalry underscored by the beef between rappers Biggie and Tupac. Especially since Tupac was killed on the Strip in 1996. As a result, any artist connected to Bad Boy was mandated by Las Vegas Metro to have extra officers present at their show.

We only had two days before the event, and I had to come up with an extra $4,000. Out of the blue, Floyd paged me to check-in and find out how my 112 concert was going. I congratulated him on improving his record to 21-0. He won his 3rd title defense in a ninth round knockout over Justin Juuko. I gave him the rundown about the extra security costs I was faced with. He told me to stay put, he had something for me.

It took him about fifteen minutes to pull up at the Soup and Salad restaurant I was eating at with Aaron. He handed me four separate stacks of $1,000 each wrapped in one rubber band. This is how he did things. Cash was always wrapped in smaller increments, and then banded in one big wad together.

We barely broke even for the show, and I couldn't give Floyd his money back. He was salty for months, to the extent that we didn't even speak when we saw each other. When we did see each other, his friend Shaun said "hello," while Floyd looked passed me, and only acknowledge Ebony.

We started speaking again later that summer. Floyd wanted to partner with me on another party at the Drink nightclub that winter. He put up $2,000 of his own money and I was able to match his contribution with a $2,000 sponsorship. My plan was to make all of his money back. I wanted to give him the $4,000 from the 112 party, plus what he put in for this one.

We had a profitable night in that we met the $15,000 bar guarantee, and netted a few extra dollars. It felt good to be able to give Floyd $6,000, but I was frustrated that Kevin, Aaron, and I took home nothing. They were upset, but understood I was trying to structure a relationship that would eventually pay off for all of us. Making good with Floyd for his previous investment was absolutely necessary.

The next day, Floyd called me over to his house and ended up giving me half of the money. He called us even. He had no idea Kevin and I really needed that money to cover our household bills.

By the time late fall rolled around, I landed a gig on a television series being shot in Vegas called, "The Strip." I was working as an extra along with my girl Christi. Floyd paged me at 2:00 a.m. while I was still on set. He made it seem like I had to come over right away to pick-up something important at his house. It was a cell phone. Not any cell phone, it was the big ass yellow Nextel with the chirp. He wore that chirp out! I could be anywhere and hear, "Tasha where you at? Tasha, Tasha, it's Floyd." He called or chirped to get my attention whenever he wanted.

That year, I was also in training to be a flight attendant for American Airlines. I was based out of Chicago. Whether I was in Texas, or Chicago, I answered whenever he chirped. He wasn't just keeping tabs on me; he hired me as a consultant to get Philthy Rich off the ground.

I rented a crash pad in Chicago. My roommates Jamie and Shamella knew everything that was going on. They found the chirp and Floyd comically entertaining. We were like the stories to them. They couldn't wait until I came through the door from a trip so they could get the next update.

Working with Floyd was definitely a hustle. I was looking to build a permanent working relationship with Floyd as a means to financial independence. I imagine that's not too far-off from the actions of women working in the corporate sector. Financial independence can be attained through college degrees, climbing the corporate ladder, or through working for a millionaire. They're all hustles.

ROUND 1: RING THE BELL

In 2002, I oscillated between a 9-5 as a medical biller for an OB/GYN, and my growing responsibilities of starting a record label with Floyd. I was still building my roster as a manager which solely consisted of my girlfriend CeCe. She was signed-up to sing in the annual *Business of the Music* talent showcase in Vegas sponsored by 88.1 KCEP. After her performance, she was approached by Jay King of Club Nouveau, and music industry marketing heavyweight, Kevin "Black" Collins, for a follow-up meeting.

Black, as he was known in the industry, was a heavyweight in every sense of the word. He was over 300 pounds, and talked with a gruff rap cadence. Hailing from the Throgs Neck section of the Bronx, New York, Black was comfortable holding his own in front of people.

He was a verbose man who expressed himself using a certain *colorful* language. The man spoke like he was rhythmically moving a crowd. No matter what we were talking about, his favorite phrase for me would make its way into the conversation, "Tasha, Tasha, let's get this muthafucka! No bullshitting." He used his swollen hands like he was a conductor.

He started his career as a DJ before becoming a senior executive at Death Row Records. Black was credited for executive producing Snoop's *Doggy Style* and was the Executive Vice-President of Rap at Def Jam Records when we met.

Jay King brought additional music industry credibility to the meeting. He was a founding member of Timex Social Club and started Club Nouveau when that group broke up. They won a Grammy for their remake of Bill Weather's *Lean on Me*. When executives of that kind of pedigree express interest, you have to take the meeting no matter where it's called to take place.

CeCe is a strong, centered woman, who happened to be petite and attractive. She had better sense than to go to their hotel room alone. She called to see if I was available to accompany her. It was a Sunday afternoon, time I normally reserved for my family. The music business is a time thief. In order to become successful, you have to be willing to drop what you're doing to take advantage of an opportunity. I changed my plans and drove to the Luxor to meet up with them. The conference was held at the pyramid shaped hotel that featured a light beam visible 275 miles in the sky.

We made our way up to their hotel room so CeCe could sing a few more songs and get feedback from Black and Jay. I couldn't tell if Black was serious about doing any business until I mentioned I was starting a record label with Pretty Boy Floyd. The tone of the conversation changed completely. Black rolled his eyes, threw his hands up, and sighed incredulously.

He had a lot of negative things to say about athletes starting labels. He was skeptical of their ability to run a business. He professed the only credible label an athlete presided over was Shaq's because he was hands-on and working with the business. This guy was so full of himself, in an affable way. Jay mostly sat back and listened. The two of them were good friends and obviously he'd seen Black's *show* before.

Black challenged me to get Floyd to come to the hotel right then and there. Floyd was with his manager, Leonard Ellerbe, on his way to church. But as soon as I called him, he turned his car around and headed our way. Leonard had ascended the ranks with Floyd going back to the first year he turned pro. He was a trainer, assistant, and on his way to becoming one of Floyd's primary business advisors. His shaded prescription glasses made it difficult for me to look him in the eye.

When Floyd arrived, I gave Black pause for doubting me. That happens a lot in the music industry. Women, especially, aren't given a fair shake. Male executives believe they're the only people on earth who have connections. By the time Floyd arrived, everybody was hungry. It was Sunday and only fitting that we sat down for Sunday supper.

We broke bread at Kathy's Southern Cooking Restaurant, a staple in Henderson, a suburb of Las Vegas. Kathy's was a small, family run place. When you opened the door, you were greeted by the snaps of the oil in the fryer. I smelled the house spices that were accented with Lawry's seasoned salt and some closely guarded family blends. They had a tiny kitchen that pumped out the crispiest, most well-seasoned wings, and the juiciest chops. Their sides were so good, at times I went there just to order a three item veggie plate of yams, greens and fried okra. We loved this place.

We left the restaurant and shuttled Black around between Floyd's house and the Philthy Rich studio. Jay had long gone on his way and Black called Stephanie, his colleague from Clive Davis' J Records, to join us at Floyd's house. Black pulled me aside and pointed out "If he wants to really make it big in this music industry, he's gonna have to spend some money, but I will support him. He needs to be in Puerto Rico for the *Mix Show Power Summit* this Wednesday." This was an important conference for radio DJs and anyone trying to get their music played on the radio.

The short notice was a challenge, but I knew I had to make it happen. We had a product to promote in Puerto Rico since Philthy Rich signed rapper Earl Hayes, who was managed by Shaun "Head" Tyler. He was the same Shaun who was trying to sneak into Club Utopia with Floyd on the night we met. I wasn't sure if we could get everyone there in time.

Floyd had me book seven tickets for himself, Earl Hayes, Shaun, his cousin Dejuan, Leonard, his sister Tawanna, and me. I was working at the OB/GYN office, managing the Philthy Rich studio, and still networking in the industry. Two of those things I could do in Puerto Rico. It wasn't going to be easy to get out of my shift at the OB's office. Tawanna had a day job too. She was working at Ford Motor Credit. We both ended up telling our boss a lie to get out of work for half the week. We weren't going to pass up a free trip to Puerto Rico.

The *Mix Show Power Summit* was a big deal. Everyone was there: Trina, Missy Elliot, Timbaland, Rasheeda and us! There was an up-and-coming New York City based rapper everyone was buzzing about. He had been on a few mix tapes and was supposed to be the next big thing. Floyd was familiar with underground music; way more than I was. He needed no introduction to the music of Curtis Jackson, AKA 50 Cent.

We went from the *Business of the Music Conference* in Vegas to the *Mix Show Power Summit* in Puerto Rico in a matter of three days. My life with Floyd was either moving at the speed of lightning, or stagnant. I tuned out anything that wasn't right in front of me. That included Kevin. I hadn't picked up a call from him in a few hours. I wasn't ignoring him intentionally. I just knew I had to focus. My plan was to call him later in the evening when I could give him my full attention.

Black signed 50 and Eminem to Interscope Records. Eminem's movie 8 *Mile* premiered while we were in Puerto Rico. Everywhere we went, Black was in somebody's ear talking about how 50 was about to blow up.

He was also in my ear coaching me about how to accelerate Philthy Rich. I knew Floyd was serious. He was at every seminar, front and center, with pen and pad. I was right by his side. Nobody could tell me that we weren't going to make it. We were an independent label with a hungry team of artists and decision makers. With Floyd's drive and my experience we had a winning combination.

We spent Wednesday through Sunday at the Westin Rio, a five-star resort, in Fajardo. At one of the parties, Black made the formal introduction between Floyd and 50. Tawanna and I snickered under our breath after she greeted him. Earlier that day, we went swimming and she had her hair wrapped in a scarf. After she got out of the water, the fabric was hard to ring out and took on a funky, damp, mildew smell. It straight-up stank. We just knew 50 got a strong whiff of odor from that scarf around her neck when he was hugging her.

50 had swag. He embodied the DNA of a rapper from New York City. He had a sculptured physique and was an alpha male in whatever room he entered. He and Floyd were similar in their laser focus and intense drive to be wildly successful. They became good friends and confidents.

Floyd came out of his comfort zone and we all saw a different side to him during this trip. We were at a banquet where Petey Pablo performed his song *North Carolina*. Petey was doing his trademark move of standing on the tables, taking his shirt off, and swinging it around the top of his head with one hand. Out of nowhere, Floyd joined him. He was starting to show his spontaneous side. For someone who didn't drink or smoke, he could be all out wild and unpredictable. I was watching the Floyd Mayweather brand evolve from an athlete to an entertainer.

Black pulled me aside again before we left Puerto Rico. "Tasha, where do you fit in all of this? I mean, have you secured yourself in his company?" I didn't really know where he was going with his questioning. We were having fun and I assumed Floyd was going to do right by me. It was because of me that we were in this mix in the first place. He declared, "If this label works or not, he's a boxer, he will make money. His boy, Leonard, is tied into the boxing paychecks. Earl Hayes is an artist, they come and go. Dejuan and Tawanna are family; he'll always take care of them. Tasha where do you stand? Where is your security with Floyd?" I had always considered myself to be a loyal and honest person. Eventually, I thought that would be enough to equate to real currency with Floyd. I told Black I was willing to wait my turn.

Black almost sounded like my husband. The two of them were similar in a couple of ways. I was married to Kevin White who was born September 29th. My friend, Kevin Black, was born September 28th. Kevin's birthday happened to fall while we were in Puerto Rico. In my absence, my mother and my Aunt Geraldine bought Kevin a cake and made sure they spent time with him. They suspected it could get under his skin that I was in Puerto Rico, with a bunch of dudes instead of home with him.

We all had cell phones, but only mine worked on the island for some reason. Whenever someone had to make a call, they used my phone. Floyd needed it a couple of times to call his girlfriend, Josie Harris, to check on her. I wouldn't say they were on the verge of marriage, but he was committed to her. She stayed behind because she was in the third trimester of her pregnancy with their youngest daughter, Jirah. They already had two boys, Koraun, and Zion. Floyd and his previous girlfriend, Melissia, had a daughter named Iyanna who was just months younger than Koraun.

On Kevin's birthday night, Josie didn't pick up the call. I had already spoken to Kevin, so instead of Floyd staying in our room trying to reach Josie, I let him take my phone next door to his suite.

I was awoken the next morning by a knock on the door. Leonard was there with my phone saying Kevin was on the line. All I could manage to say was "hello" before he started screaming at me.

He accused me of being in bed with Floyd because why else would he answer my phone. When I explained what was going on, he insisted that I was lying and hung up. He should've heard the footsteps of people walking the phone around and doors opening and closing. I remember being stunned and hurt that he didn't seem to trust me at all.

Kevin completely changed his life when he moved from Atlanta to Vegas to be with me, so I gave him a lot of leeway to express his feelings. His dreams of becoming a singer and continuing his dancing career had to be sacrificed when we had Jaelin. I admired his will to take care of our family, and felt guilty for asking him to be in the background of my own pursuit in the industry. I knew we would make-up when I got home.

In the airport, Tawanna and I had a star-struck groupie episode. We had just left a resort full of celebrities where neither of us was particularly shook by any of them. We squealed like school girls when we spotted Kamar de los Reyes, who played Antonio Vega on *One Life to Live*. He was our favorite star on the stories. Floyd was so annoyed, but I didn't care one bit if he was embarrassed. Antonio was fine. Floyd teased us for a while after that.

I tried to keep the momentum going after Puerto Rico. We arranged to fly 50 to town to perform in a show at the Vegas Sports Park. Our rap artists Dirt Bomb, HFLO, and Earl Hayes opened for him. We had a few subsequent meetings with Black in an effort to produce a Philthy Rich compilation album. Floyd kept stalling and never made a decision on moving forward.

Black stayed in my ear cautioning me to find other opportunities within Floyd's business. He didn't think we would be a successful label while Floyd was making all of the major decisions. He said he wasn't hungry for the music industry. He had plenty of money and was already a celebrity in his own right. He was basically telling me what others had told me in the past. I wasn't ready to listen to them or Black. I believed in my ability and had the patience to convince Floyd to make the best decisions concerning Philthy Rich.

Friends who were decision makers in the industry started to question Floyd's motives for being involved in the label. This was underscored when I scheduled a meeting with my good friend Kawan "KP" Prather, and Philthy Rich Rapper, HFLO. KP agreed to the meeting based on our working relationship that went back to my days with LaFace. Floyd didn't attend the meeting. Instead, he sent his manager Leonard and sister Tawanna with me.

Floyd had HFLO dripping in diamonds and gold jewelry. His appearance was off putting to KP. He felt like there was way too much flash and too little substance. KP was completely honest when he commented that HFLO was already wearing his whole marketing budget on him.

If Floyd spent this amount of money on his artist before they even sold one record, KP felt his involvement would be irrelevant. He turned us away saying, "Floyd had the money to do whatever he needed to do." I was glad Tawanna and Leonard heard this information. I already expressed that Floyd was spending too much money on the image of our artists. He'd brush me off by saying, "Money is no problem."

I became more aware of his disconnect while meeting with Kevin Liles and Lyor Cohen. Kevin Liles was the Executive Vice President of Island Def Jam Music Group from 1999-2004. He was responsible for crossing over artist like LL Cool J, Kanye West, and Ludacris. He was a brand and marketing expert.

Lyor Cohen had been Run DMC's road manager and eventually formed Rush Records with Russell Simmons. The two of them were responsible for tens of millions of records being sold and launched dozens of careers. My contact, Jerry Stokes, called to see if Floyd would sit down with them. Floyd didn't want to meet them in New York. He wanted to send me on his behalf since he was a bit skeptical of Jerry's intentions.

Jerry was cool with me, so I took the initial meeting anyway.

Liles and Cohen proposed a joint venture with Floyd. They pitched an idea to release a workout DVD in exchange for a distribution deal with Philthy Rich records. We'd produce the music and they would get it sold through their various channels. I thought the arrangement was a win-win; I was excited to get Floyd in front of these guys.

When I took their proposal to him, Leonard didn't want to do the deal. He thought Floyd could produce his own DVD without having to give someone else a cut of the profits. I was a team player and went along with Leonard, but having the support of a label like Def Jam distributing our music would have made my life easier.

Leonard and I didn't disagree about much when it came to business matters. We made sure not to double book Floyd for our respective engagements. I stayed in the entertainment lane and he stayed in the boxing lane.

I really didn't know much about Leonard personally. Neither did Floyd. He shared very limited informal information with us other than the fact that he grew up in D.C. It wasn't out of the ordinary for Floyd not to have personal information on people who worked for him. Leonard was different though. He was part of the inner-circle. Yet, we had no idea where lived, or how he spent his free time.

On the occasions when we did bump heads, Floyd definitely encouraged the discord. He said he wanted to create competition in the camp. "I'm going to have everybody fighting for their position," he confessed one night at the office.

Sometimes, I didn't feel like it was much of a fight if my point of view was different from Leonard's. Floyd didn't always think Leonard was right, but he gave greater credibility to advice coming from a man. I had as much, or more experience in entertainment as Leonard did in boxing. Still, I had more to prove because I was a woman in a world dominated by men.

The artists were frustrated by having the release of their music delayed. They were tired of waiting while their projects sat on the Philthy Rich shelf. The delay wasn't always Floyd's fault. Some of them got caught up in materialism and admiration of Floyd's lifestyle, when they should've been getting busy in the studio. Metaphorically, everyone had their lane; how they drove their car was really their choice. Some followed Floyd blindly, and so closely that when he stopped they crashed. If he switched lanes, they lost him.

Floyd's friend Shaun made sure his artist Earl Hayes maintained forward progress, but was managing him with very little success at Philthy Rich. He made a move to sign Earl to Interscope without discussing it with Floyd first. Hayes was still contractually bound to Philthy Rich and had to be released first. Although his friendship with Shaun suffered some, they started speaking again since Floyd made money on the deal.

Floyd had his own agenda. He needed to maintain control and ownership of everything; a mindset that doomed a lot of business deals. I tried harder to bring him opportunities thinking eventually we'd find something he'd sign off on. I figured it was a numbers game--the more I tried, the more likely I'd be successful.

Lesson 1: Empathy Is Your Pedigree

We're all connected as human beings by a thread of empathy. Anything good or impressive in our history is related to how we've treated others. The thought of caring about other people was contradictory in the cutthroat world of boxing. I tried to introduce Floyd to the concept that reaching the top of the music business required cultivating relationships and maintaining professional and personal contacts.

I was able to connect with KP, Kevin Liles, and Lyor Cohen because I respected their experience and valued their time. Empathy allowed me to break down barriers and open a lot of doors to places I wouldn't otherwise have access to.

ROUND 2: BLURRED VISION

2003 was a watershed year in my life. The music industry was starting to buzz about Floyd, his new label, and the artists we'd signed. What began as a promotions partnership between Floyd and me, evolved into a branding and marketing role. I knew I was an asset, not some stray he rescued. We worked well together. Floyd was gifted at getting people to pay attention to him whenever he opened his mouth, and he opened his mouth a lot.

I was indoctrinated with his personal philosophy of value. He valued money and the loyalty he was able to purchase with it. Sadly, Floyd associated love with loyalty as if one equated the other. His attitude made sense, considering the fact that he grew up in an environment that didn't offer much trust or loyalty. While being interviewed for the Ricky Hatton fight, he told a UK reporter, "I had a father who was a hustler and a mother who was on drugs. I was the man in the house from 16. That's just the way it was."

He frequently mentioned, when people acquired money the first thing they did was get new teeth. I saw this while I was working as a dental billing assistant with Dr. Garnhardt. Floyd was always intrigued by entrepreneurs. He was drawn to individuals who wrote their own checks.

He would pull up in the Philthy Rich van followed by two or three Mercedes' bumpin' loud rap music. I knew everybody in the office was looking at me like I was bringing in the riff-raff. He was cool with Dr. Garnhardt though. They talked about the business side of the practice, like how he found patients, and what it took to become profitable. It seemed like Dr. Garnhardt enjoyed talking with Floyd.

In his own way Floyd showed respect for Dr. Garnhardt's time. He didn't just come to the office to hang out. He persuaded his homeboy Tom to get some dental work done, and paid Dr. Garnhardt $10,000 in cash for his services.

Floyd was free spirited and fun. He wanted me around and I liked feeling valued. From time to time, he surprised me with expensive designer handbags in addition to cash to compensate me for my work. Not consistently, just enough to keep my nose open.

I was able to transfer all I had learned at LaFace

Records into my work at Philthy Rich. I concentrated on artist development as the foundation of the label. I wrote bios, created press kits, and scheduled photo shoots for Floyd and our roster.

I hired a small staff which included our engineer Corey Harris. Officially, I was the studio's General Manager, although I wore many hats in those days. When the phone rang, I answered it using a pseudonym, pretending to be the receptionist. When I got on the call, I could change up and say, "Are you on hold for the general manager? This is Tasha."

Back at home Kevin was hanging out way past midnight that year. A few times, he didn't come home until the sun came up. Going to the studio was my escape from feeling abandoned by my husband.

When things were going really well in my career, my marriage would suffer and vice versa. It was as if Kevin and Floyd were competing to be the alpha dog in my life. Tension between my husband and my boss changed the course of my relationships at home and at work.

Initially, Kevin's biggest gripe was Floyd's inconsistent payroll schedule. We weren't on one. It was more like I had to be around all the time and hope he would drop some cash in my account. The issue ballooned, and Kevin soon demanded that I choose where my loyalty lay--either with him, or with Floyd. I thought my husband and I had love, something much greater than loyalty.

He also resented Floyd's dominance of my time. Though Kevin was more expressive about the rivalry, Floyd contributed to it in a passive aggressive fashion by the unorthodox way he ran his business. On the one hand, he'd call my phone at 4:00 a.m. and say, "Apologize to your husband for me for calling you at this time." Yet, he wouldn't stop calling at that time.

Admittedly, I allowed Floyd to establish a pattern of late night calls. I took those calls at 2:00 a.m., 3:00 a.m., and 4:00 a.m., knowing that they upset Kevin. I also knew I might not be able to reach Floyd at 11:00 in the morning. His sleeping time was between 6:00 a.m. and 3:00 p.m. If I needed him to answer a question or do anything between those hours, I was generally out of luck.

In April of 2003, Floyd called me to meet him at Diversity Tattoo a reputable tattoo and piercing establishment on the Vegas strip. I knew if I didn't get up there right away, I might have to wait a few more weeks for any compensation. This was part of the dysfunction of working for him. I'd drop whatever I was doing for the carrot he was dangling in front of me that day. On this day, it was $2,500. He was chewing on Red Vines as he handed me an envelope with the cash.

Once he left, Diversity was empty with the exception of my girl who worked there. She was still energized by his visit. She let me know Floyd left a $200 credit on the account. "You should get something done," she told me playfully. My face lit up. "Tattoo? Nope." I got my nipples pierced with that credit and let her know I planned on seducing my husband that night.

My girlfriend, Ms. Kristie, was babysitting Jaelin. The house was completely ours. I had candles and scented oil by the bed. In the background the CD player was softly going through a medley of Mint Condition's *Pretty Brown Eyes*, BBD's *When will I see you Smile Again* and of course a few songs by Guy. I couldn't wait to surprise Kevin. I almost gave up waiting until he showed up around 3:00 a.m. I would've been mad that he came home so late, but I was still hyped to surprise Kevin. I was revealing my studded twins and telling him how erotic I was feeling when the conversation took a very wrong turn.

"Floyd got your nipples pierced, Tasha? You let him

see you naked!" Oh, my God. He ignored everything else I mentioned about going to Diversity to pick up money, or the fact that Floyd was long gone before I got the piercings. He was locked in on something that didn't happen. Kevin ripped the phone out of the wall and snatched my cell from my hand during the argument.

I felt sick to my stomach when he yanked me off the bed so hard I fell to the floor and the wind was knocked out of me. When I gained my footing, I ran shoeless into the dark. I didn't stop running until I reached the Vonn's supermarket not far down the block.

I didn't have any money except for a few coins in my front pocket. I used the spare change at a payphone to call my brother Kahil. I was crushed when he told me, "Tasha, if you're not going to leave him, then I can't get involved. That's between ya'll." In the space of an hour, two of the four men I counted on the most in life had abandoned me.

I needed to feel safe and protected. My next call was to Floyd. He didn't pick up, so I left a long sobbing message for him and Leonard. Out of money and out of ideas, I had no choice but to shamefully head back home. I packed a few things and headed over to

Kristie's place.

By the time I returned home with Jaelin the next morning, Floyd had already called my cell phone a few times. He left a voicemail encouraging me to be strong and promised to help me find an apartment if I wanted to leave Kevin. For many years, I excused Floyd's behavior because of all the times he'd showed up for me when I needed help. I rationalized it the way drug addicts rationalize their addiction. Floyd Mayweather happened to be my opiate of choice.

I had no idea that Kevin answered my phone the second time Floyd called back. Each of them accused the other of being unstable and controlling. I was afraid the situation was going to get blown way out of proportion. It only took a couple of days for them to meet in a crowded Las Vegas nightclub. From what they both relayed to me, they headed straight toward one another, fully expecting a physical altercation. Floyd's entourage broke the two of them up before things escalated to the point of punches being thrown. Indirectly, Kevin was part of the Mayweather family. This was family business, and didn't need to be handled in the streets.

Kevin and I resided under the same roof while living separate lives. I thought about leaving him because I didn't want to be a woman trapped in an unhealthy relationship. So much of our history involved distrust and contempt. We were on the verge of being in a state of disrepair. Being able to provide for Jaelin became my number one priority. I wanted her to see her mother as a strong, capable woman.

We gained clarity and perspective about what was important in life a couple of weeks later when we found out our good friend, Lisa "Left Eye" Lopes, of the group TLC was killed in a car accident. Kevin and I eventually made amends, but I wasn't able to undo the damage to the relationship between my boss and my husband. That was permanent.

I regret calling Floyd. I put Kevin in a terrible position. From that day on Floyd knew he had me. The perfect picture of home I tried to paint was forever tarnished. We had more than work between us. We were friends who genuinely looked out for one another. Floyd knew I needed help and now he could rescue me too.

Lesson 2: Stagger and Stand

You don't stop being a champion because you get knocked down; you are a champion because you get back up. In my case, when my marriage was at its lowest point, I had to summon the courage to try again because I believed we were worth the effort. Counseling, the strength of our family, and our faith in prayer helped us change how we dealt with hard-times within our marriage.

I realize some women are in unhealthy relationships that require them to leave and seek help immediately. Sometimes getting up has to be accompanied by getting out. If you or anyone you know is a victim of domestic violence please call the National Domestic Violence Helpline. Trained advocates are available to take your calls through a toll-free, 24/7 hotline at 1-800-799-SAFE (7233). You can also visit the website at www.thehotline.org.

ROUND 3: THE UNDERCARD

Some people want a job that pays them well. I wanted a job that allowed me to pay whatever I got forward. When I saw Floyd looking out for strangers, it meant more than my boss doing a nice thing. I took these acts of kindness personally. Floyd had a soft spot for people in need, as he exhibited in the case of the man we came to know as OG, short for Original Gangsta.

The Philthy Rich Records office wasn't in the safest part of town. It was located on East Charleston in Las Vegas, in a gritty, less developed urban area. In the early days, I was usually there alone from 10 a.m.-6 p.m. The office was a ghost town. Usually, the crew spilled into the studio in the early evening. The Philthy Rich team was similar to most music industry folks I knew. They seemed to get their creative juices flowing after the sun went down.

My introduction to OG was unusual and typical of the Mayweather environment. One early fall evening, I heard a knock on the door, as I was gathering my things to leave. It was dark, and nobody I knew would pop up before calling first. The entrance was set off to the side of the street. People passing by couldn't see anything happening in the roughly constructed, eight vehicle parking lot.

Reluctantly, I cracked the door open. A scruffy vagrant greeted me with a half-coked smile. "Hello, Tasha is Floyd here?" Huh, how'd he know my name? He told me Floyd had something for him and he was there to pick it up. Now, I'd like to think that I'm capable of not judging a book by its cover. I also wasn't foolish enough to keep the door swung opened for a stranger at night. I let him know I was going to call Floyd and find out. I made sure to step backwards while closing the door as I was still talking.

When I got Floyd on the phone, he laughed and instructed me to, "Go in the back and give him some snacks. Tell him to come back a little later to see me." I was so pissed because he knew I was already a scaredy-cat when it came to being in the office alone. I didn't need a stranger calling me by name from a dark parking lot. I gave him a few bags of chips and some of the Red Vines from Floyd's private stash.

When I returned around 10:30ish that evening, the studio was packed with the usual suspects. There were a few artists in each of the two small recording booths performing for each other, and their audience of women for the night. As long as I had been around the music business I was still perplexed by groupies in the studio. Groupies didn't have to be just women either. Men would also come around just wanting to hang out and be on the scene.

Tucked away on one of the leather couches in the lounge area was an older gentleman whom I hadn't seen before. He caught my eye because he was so nicely dressed. His hair was even laid extra-crispy nice like he was fresh from the barber's chair.

Floyd gestured towards the unfamiliar man, "Tasha you remember OG, from earlier today." I shook my head no. I didn't know this man. Floyd grinned and told me I gave him snacks earlier in the evening. He cleaned OG up beyond a spit shine polish. Floyd bought him new clothes, and Floyd's barber gave him a fresh cut, and shave. But, that wasn't all. He reserved a room for him at the Budget Suites down the street. OG looked good, smelled good, and was newly employed. Floyd hired him to clean the studio and answer phones when I wasn't there.

For all I knew, OG could have been running from the law, or some kind of addict. He was all in our mix and nobody thought to check this dude out. At times, Floyd extended himself to people as if they had no past. All that mattered for him was the present. As if what was immediately at hand was the driving force for what he chose to do. He extended himself to OG in this way. Sometimes I admired this quality in him. Having the means to do good for others doesn't necessarily mean people choose to do so. When Floyd did, I was more than willing to be supportive even when I had suspicions about the people he helped out.

He asked me to get his family's information in order to let them know OG was okay and part of the Philthy Rich team. I did as he asked, and his people seemed to be grateful. So did OG. I noticed that Floyd never gave him money, he provided him with food, a comfy place to stay, and clothes in exchange for the work he did around the studio.

Floyd allowed OG to walk him into the ring along with his Philthy Rich crew into for what became win number 30 against Victoriano Sosa. He rolled in with a matching Adidas sweat suit that had Philthy Rich on it. OG looked like he was going to the gym for a work out.

He was probably around for about eight months or so. After OG failed to show up to clean the studio one day, Floyd explained he had a habit and apparently had fallen off the wagon. Over the years, I watched Floyd use his money and influence for both good and well, not so good.

He could be especially generous around the holidays. One year, Floyd and Josie gifted a Christian Dior, Gucci, or Louis Vuitton bag to every female friend and family member who stopped by the house on Christmas Eve.

I never knew what to get him for Christmas or birthdays because I knew he could buy anything he wanted. I decided to give him gifts from the heart. I bought him books like *Make it Happen* by Kevin Liles and *Do You* by Russell Simmons because I thought they would resonate with him personally. I noticed they were displayed on his bookshelf whenever he moved.

I was enjoying my job and I like being around Floyd. Nothing was the same from one day to the next. My job responsibilities grew to include going to the bank with him to shuffle money off to people he was taking care of. He often put money on the books of friends in prison back in Grand Rapids, and across the country.

We went everywhere together. He even added me to his auto insurance plan just in case I ever needed to drive one of his cars.

We were grinding. We needed to find artists to sign to the label. He wanted me to fly in a singer/rapper named Jumbo he knew from Grand Rapids. I briefly wondered if he was my friend J Rock from my Lansing talent show days. When I set up the flights, I had to reserve the ticket under Jumbo's government name, James Owens. It seemed familiar to me, but I still couldn't place him.

When he arrived, I couldn't believe James was indeed J Rock from my talent show days. He spent his summers merely forty-five minutes away from Lansing in Grand Rapids. He went by J Rock in Lansing and Jumbo in Grand Rapids. We were excited by the thought of linking up these two Michigan boys. Unfortunately, neither of them could agree on the terms of a contract. They remained friends.

The Philthy Rich office became my safety zone. It gave me someplace to go and plenty to do. I was managing a girl group called Ebonired. Eboni, Tekiya "Teka," Toya, and Trina were my reinvention of Xscape. I learned the blueprint of how to assemble talent from Ian Burke in Atlanta. Eboni and Trina lived in Vegas while Toya and Teka resided in Atlanta. All of them had some industry experience. In fact, Toya was coming off a gig singing background vocals on an up and coming rapper's track. You know him today as T.I.

They were all beautiful and talented which made it easy to persuade Floyd to give them free studio time. The girls worked with some great producers like Stokely Watson and Michael Mcclain, dad to China Mcclain, star of Disney's hit show A.N.T. Farm.

Floyd wanted to sign Ebonired and didn't hold back on flashing his money in front of them. In addition to giving them free studio time, he loaned them fur coats for their first photo shoot. He also asked his girlfriend, Josie, to do their make-up for the day. For the most part, when we needed money, we worked for it. Floyd would have given us cash if I had asked him. I never wanted to when it came to the girls.

I had them set-up a car wash to pay for their

outfits. I couldn't win for losing though. Floyd showed up with all of his cars that afternoon. He had his staff drive over the Maybach, Rolls, and every Mercedes he owned at the time. He shut down our carwash and paid us to work on his fleet all day.

I operated with the duality of Ebonired's manager and employee of the label. I had been keeping a close eye on the progression of Earl Hayes. I resolved that Ebonired wasn't going to end up owing Philthy Rich, or Floyd for anything.

Floyd personally got Ebonired approved to sing the National Anthem on the evening of his first fight with Jose Luis Castillo at the MGM Grand Arena. It was hard not to be affected by the electricity generated around fight night. Being around him made you feel like a celebrity.

We stayed overnight in the MGM to be close to the arena. It's one of the largest casinos in the world known for its emerald green exterior. For Floyd, that color was money green. I couldn't walk a single step without seeing a reference to the Mayweather fight. Without a doubt Floyd's star was on the rise. The pinging sounds of slot machines followed us all the way to the elevators.

I left the girls to prepare in their room while I attended a meet and greet on behalf of his boxing promotions company, then known as Pretty Boy Enterprises. Leonard was preoccupied with Floyd's fight logistics. They sent me to mingle with the likes of Evander Holyfield, Richard Steele, George Foreman, and HBO head honcho, Ross Greenburg. I was the only female at the table with these boxing deities until Kelly Swanson, his boxing publicist, arrived. I had exclusive access to the *boys club* of boxing.

His win over Castillo, albeit one of his most controversial to date was a win for me as well. The girls gained a greater respect for me as their manager. They knew I could put them in a situation to become stars.

I was conscious about being a role model for them. We were surrounded by philandering, loud talking men. In order to hold my own, I showed up to work on time and I handled my business while I was there. Most importantly, I made sure I went home to my family every night. Despite my best efforts and the resources we had access to, the group broke up.

At home, Kevin and I were slowly repairing our relationship through the summer months. He bought me so many bouquets of pink and white lilies, I told him to save his money. (He hasn't bought me any since.) In Vegas, it was over a hundred degrees in the shade at night, and equally as hot in our bedroom.

I've heard that important news comes in threes. I met Kevin on July 3rd, 1990. I found out that I was pregnant with Jaelin on July 3rd, 1995. On July 3rd, 2003, I found out that I was pregnant with our son.

I didn't tell Floyd immediately because I didn't want him to take any of my responsibilities away. I waited until late August to tell him and Leonard. I don't think they believed me at first as I didn't start to show until later in my second trimester.

Jaelin was about to turn eight, and I took her to Mommy and Me classes to help her prepare to be a big sister. I was praying that my kids would be as close as I was to Lawrence and Kahil. Jaelin was a child with an independent spirit. From a young age, she displayed a passion for the arts, especially dancing. She literally followed her father's footsteps into the entertainment world. She was a dancer for Future Shock, a youth oriented dance group based in Vegas. She practiced hard and was a good teammate. I knew she would look out for her baby brother.

Kevin was the doting dad-to-be, rubbing my feet and placating any food cravings I had. The anticipation of our baby boy further strengthened our commitment to our marriage. Still, it was a difficult time for me. My parents had unexpectedly divorced after 33 years of marriage.

My brothers and I were devastated as if we were ten years old. We cried in disbelief, and the three of us made a pact that we would never be divorced. The pain I felt absolutely effected how I viewed my own marriage. I swore I would marry one person and work out our problems no matter what.

I was already hormonal due to my pregnancy, so I took their decision especially hard. Thankfully, I didn't experience any morning sickness. Certain behavior made me sick though. My tolerance level was dissipating. I noticed that the more Floyd transitioned his public persona from *Pretty Boy* into *Money*, the more my charming, fur coat wearing friend morphed into a vociferous bully.

He barked a lot at the studio. The two of us started to constantly beef about the business. The arguing became untenable when I was trying to tell him how to set an appropriate budget. He shouted, "I'm the Puffy of this label! You just answer phones!" He embarrassed me in front of the group of guys who were in the studio that night. I immediately walked out the door and didn't return to work for Floyd.

Sure, I was sensitive due to my pregnancy, but I wasn't about to be disrespected. I heard the words of Kevin Black in the back of my mind. Nobody had released a single and I was tired of turning down offers from legitimate labels. Floyd was telling me we could be a completely independent label. "We" was too many people. He wanted to be completely independent. The rest of us were at his mercy.

Right around this time, Kevin took a job offer with a telecommunications company located in Africa. I was six months pregnant. So, he had to leave me behind with Jaelin. He came home to be with us just before our son was born, one day after his sister's birthday, March 2, 2004. Jaelin was adamant about two things on that day. I needed to me to bring cupcakes to her classroom, and her brother was not to be born on her birthday.

She got her wishes. I made it to her school and spent 24 hours enduring contractions and labor pains mostly at home. I went to the hospital twice in that timeframe. I lost my mucus plug, but my water didn't break. Apparently, I wasn't dilated enough for them to keep me.

Having a baby is difficult, emotional, excruciatingly painful, and like many moms will tell you somewhat comical. My prolonged labor wasn't funny at all. At home, I knelt by the side of my couch in agony. I tried to concentrate on my breathing while grabbing at things that weren't even there until the contractions passed. I think I might've cussed myself out a few times. "Oh, my god, won't this baby come already!" I screamed in one of those quiet, teeth clenched voices. I thought I was going to deliver my son right on my living room floor.

Finally, after a day of closing my eyes and squeezing my fists in the air, I decided to go back to St. Rose Hospital. I was going to deliver my son right there, in the freaking hospital, no matter what the doctors said.

In my mind, I was going to deliver our son with four pushes just like I did with Jaelin. After I pushed hard enough for the crown of his head to appear, the doctor called the delivery team to halt. What! I was ready! The baby was in distress and I had to be prepped for an emergency C-Section. I was crushed. It was important for me to deliver my baby the all-natural way. I still regret not doing so.

Kevin spent the time I was prepped for the epidural getting something to eat. I wanted to jump off of the bed and choke him out when he came into the room scarfing down food from Burger King. He didn't think twice about offering me some. The smell of crispy, greasy, golden fried goodness that I couldn't have was maddening. What was he thinking?

Payback time came when the doctors were completing my C-section. For some reason, he peeked over the tarp draped above my waist to shield us from the happenings below. My insides were wide opened and room looked like a real life episode of *Grey's Anatomy.* My chocolate skinned husband turned ghostly white. The man almost fainted.

I still don't know why *I like the way you move* by Outkast was pumping from the radio. I remember listening to the chorus, *"I like the waaaaay you move"* and hearing the faint sound of an infant interfering with the repetition of the best part of the song. I asked Kevin who brought their baby into the room. "It's your baby, Tasha. It's our son." We named him Kevin, and he would be called by his nickname, KJ.

I had to wait until KJ was three months old before the kids, my mom, and I were able to safely fly to Egypt. When we arrived, I was surprised to learn that Cairo was a city with over 18 million people. The land was layered with history. On the drive to our temporary home, I could see ruins that were thousands of years old, with influences from the British and French sprinkled in between.

We lived in an 8,500 square foot, guard-gated oasis. The company provided a private chef, drivers, and around the clock security. We were accompanied by an armed chauffeur whenever we ventured outside of our subdivision. It wasn't much different than how I traveled with Floyd. We were sheltered, yet not impervious to the political uncertainty surrounding us.

During Kevin's 10 hour shift, I spent my time home schooling Jaelin using the Calvert School curriculum to get her through third grade. Her education was enriched by the history of the city we were in.

There were four other families with young children working for the company. We tried to pool our efforts whenever possible, even though our kids were different ages. I took the kids on field trips. A highlight for them was viewing an Egyptian sarcophagus that was over 5,000 years old.

My mom was a great help while we were there. She kept me company and stayed with the kids so Kevin and I could enjoy a few date nights. We spent our ninth wedding anniversary having dinner on the Nile. While the restaurant rotated, we were able to take in the panoramic orange and red sunset. Kevin and I had been tested during our nine-year marriage. Maybe we fell down a few times, but we loved each other enough to dust ourselves off and try, and try again.

Even though they were divorced at the time, my dad joined my mom and us in Egypt. He was hilarious the first time he rode a camel at a location near the Giza Pyramids. Being in Cairo with my entire nuclear family was a dream come true. My childhood consisted of memories of my parents taking us all over the country. Now, I was able to create new memories in a part of the world none of us had ever seen before.

I prayed that mom and dad would consider their six month separation as temporary, and realize that they were meant to be together. My prayers were answered. Our trip to Egypt was such a loving experience that when my parents returned to the States, my dad asked my mom to marry him again.

I left Egypt three months after they did. My mom's oldest sister, Patricia, known to us as "Bootsie," was being laid to rest in Ohio.

When you return from another country, even the dirt in the United States looks new. My career and my marriage were experiencing a brand new start.

Lesson 3: Passion Reveals Purpose

When I returned from Egypt, I identified my real life's purpose—helping others. I knew that finding my passion in my career would allow me to fulfill that purpose.

Over the years, friends and family members have asked me why I put up with Floyd and the madness of our work situation for so long. I can't give a cut and dry answer. I can say, partially, my reason was because I saw morsels of unselfishness and humanity that persuaded me to think there was something bigger at stake than a paycheck. I wanted to contribute to the greater good. I had the passion and the purpose. He provided the platform.

ROUND 4: LISTEN TO MY COMMANDS

When I returned to Vegas in 2005, I was hired as a special events coordinator by the Silverton Casino. It was a newer, local's casino, on the expanding southern end of Las Vegas Boulevard. My move to Egypt provided both the time and space I needed to get over my abrupt departure from Floyd and Philthy Rich. When I did run into Floyd we didn't have much to say to one another. We nodded acknowledgement and kept it moving. There was no ill will or hate, just a mutual non-verbal agreement that our time together was done.

Tawanna and I stayed in touch despite my falling out with her brother. Tawanna was more than a friend. She was part of my sisterhood. She shared her honest opinion whenever Floyd gave me expensive gifts, or if I was away from home for too long. She looked at me through the lenses of her expensive glasses, (that girl kept up with designer eyeglass frames) and didn't mince words, "You're a married woman. You have a family. You shouldn't be accepting these kinds of gifts from him." I appreciated her candor. She was coming from a good place.

She really wanted the two of us to reconcile for business and personal reasons. That February, she gave Floyd a surprise birthday party at his house, and insisted I show up. After the gathering, everyone was heading to a strip club; everyone except for me. Dejuan played peacemaker, trying to convince me otherwise. "Champ wants all of you guys to come out." There was no need for me to stay mad at Floyd. I was content with my life. I decided to go out with them for a little bit.

Floyd and I spent the night playfully accusing the other of ending our relationship. He put his arm on my shoulder telling everyone within earshot that I quit. I jabbed back, "You fired me." The banter between us that evening was our way of apologizing to one another. I was back in the Mayweather fold, only this time the stakes were higher. I had a young family to provide for.

He was scheduling more public appearances in his home town. He hired me to fly in and help promote a celebrity basketball game. We were both surprised when the City of Grand Rapids honored us individually for contributions to the community. While we were standing at the podium, he leaned in and declared, "You may need to quit your other job and work exclusively for me. I'll pay you double what you're making at the Silverton."

I resolved to do things differently. I wanted an appropriate executive title and the equivalent compensation. Floyd agreed. I hoped we could start over, and let the past be the past.

I became CEO of Mayweather Music and Founding President of the Floyd Mayweather Jr. Foundation. We didn't discuss an exact compensation amount, or pay schedule. There was no use in trying to convince Floyd to create a business structure he didn't want to adhere to.

He more than doubled my Silverton salary though. I was paid a least $8,000 a month with regular bonuses of $20,000 to $100,000 at a time.

I went to the Clark County Department of Business License to purchase the business names Mayweather Music, Mayweather Promotions, Floyd Mayweather Jr. Foundation, and a few others. At the very least, we needed to own those business names. In order to make my new positions official, I contacted an attorney to set up a Limited Liability Company, (L.L.C) listing Floyd and I as partners in Mayweather Music.

I hired Beschelle Lockhart as the Executive Director of the Floyd Mayweather Jr. Foundation. She compiled all of the proper legal paperwork for us, maintained the books, and assisted in setting-up the organization's Board. She had experience working for non-profits and was a fellow Elegante' from Lansing.

I left the responsibility of corporatizing Mayweather Promotions to Floyd and Leonard. The activities under that umbrella were mostly boxing related.

Floyd paid the first year's rent in advance on our plush, customized Rancho office building. The space was nicely laid out. Floyd installed three 55 inch flat screen televisions in the waiting room. His personal office came equipped with a beautiful marble shower. I don't think he ever used it. It was there more for show. The Philthy Rich studio stayed in the East Charleston section of town.

When the time came for me to leave my day job, I gave the Silverton the customary two week notice. I was trying to wrap up outstanding projects, but Floyd was a distraction as he stopped by every day to remind me I didn't have to work there anymore. He playfully told my boss that I could leave at any time. I wanted to leave on good terms in case I needed my job back.

I transitioned from being in the studio regularly to working side by side with Floyd. He wanted me to give him my full attention. A typical day started with me getting my kids and husband to school and work respectively. Then, I was off to be with Floyd for likely the next twelve hours. We worked out a system that wasn't very efficient, but our routine made him comfortable. I was instructed to pick up mail from his mom's house, sort through the bills, and pay anything outstanding.

He gave me access to his checkbook so he didn't have to sit and write out every check for himself. He was a millionaire who spent his time making money, not accounting for it. I made copies of the bills and left them for him in a drawer by his bed. He didn't want a P.O. Box, nor did he want all of his mail delivered directly to his home. I didn't want to be responsible for his personal finances, and on more than one occasion, I suggested he hire a professional accountant, but he refused.

The inefficient handling of money became costly whenever he forgot that the bill paying account didn't have the same cushy balance as his leisure account. One day, I happened to be checking his account balance and noticed he was overdrawn. He was out shopping and pissed off that he couldn't spend whatever he wanted to spend, with any card he wanted. After he fell into the red a couple of times, I was finally able to convince him to sign up for online bill pay.

Usually, I woke him up when I got to the house. It wasn't unusual for me to find that he had company in the bedroom when I got there. Our agreement was that I had free rein to enter the bedroom as long as I knocked. I think it was more for my protection than his. Floyd had no shame in letting me see him in bed with two or three women as we started our workday. Sometimes I'd recognize the women, and sometimes I'd see new faces peeking through the covers.

Since he didn't sleep at night, I had to be flexible and roll with the schedule he wanted to maintain on any given day. When he woke up, paying bills was hardly the first thing on his mind. Every day, and I mean every day, we'd head to the bank as the first order of business. I've read a lot of rumors about Floyd Mayweather over the years and I can unequivocally confirm that this one is true. He didn't care for using plastic. Life was about having large sums of cash at his disposal at all times.

It got to the point that we had to hire a staff to support the daily operations of the Mayweather brand. Felons, strippers, and even homeless individuals had jobs in the Mayweather camp. Our assistants were no exception. Both of us had assistants who let's just say had unusual ways of securing their positions. Elena worked for me for a short while. She was a bright girl who I could count on. She was also being paid so Floyd could make good on a promise he made to her boyfriend. He was a former bodyguard for Floyd, who was serving a jail sentence at the time.

Floyd's first official assistant, Vagaz, set the bar for Mayweather job applicants. She was a well-known former stripper. At the time, she was working in Atlanta as an assistant to rapper T.I. and his wife Tiny. She met Floyd while attending a Mayweather Weekend with them in Las Vegas one summer.

Mayweather Weekends were a 48 hour period of time filled with parties and entertainment usually in

Las Vegas, or Grand Rapids. On one particular weekend, Floyd bought out a strip club for the night and hosted a $100,000 strip off. Dancers from Atlanta, Miami, and Detroit were all provided plane tickets to participate. After the contest, the party continued around Floyd's backyard pool.

Drinks were flowing (Floyd never drank), and Floyd's personal DJ had the after party in overdrive. The party got so hot that Tiny felt emboldened to ask me if I had ever slept with Floyd. I rolled my eyes, "No, I haven't. It's not like that at all." She eyeballed him, shrugged, and walked away.

Feeling especially generous, Floyd took out his famous bulging Louis Vuitton moneybag, and started raining stacks of cash in the pool. Vagaz was the prototype stripper. She was stacked from top to bottom, with long dark curly hair, and from what I observed that night was a good swimmer. She took off everything except her eyeglasses and dove all the way to the bottom of the pool like a stripper mermaid. When she came to the surface both of her hands were filled with cash.

Floyd stayed in touch with Vagaz in the weeks that followed the strip off. From what I was told, T.I. fired her. She told Floyd her boss didn't like the fact that Floyd maintained contact with her. He moved Vagaz into his house and hired her as his personal assistant.

How he lived was abnormal, but I felt like I understood him better than most people. People studied what kind of money Floyd was making and how they could benefit off of him. I studied him as a person, and I looked at his heart to find out what he wanted to do. I tell people I went to Mayweather University and studied Floyd-ology.

His blueprint for success stemmed from his mantra, "Hard work and dedication." He allowed me into his world to experience the workings of the mind of a champion during a training run. He challenged me to join him on what has now become a legendary late night five mile trek down the streets of Las Vegas. These runs were part of his training regime long before the HBO and Showtime cameras captured Floyd jogging alongside of his all-white Rolls Royce and custom Maybachs.

My pride led me to accept his challenge even though I was in no physical shape to run a couple of miles with a world-class athlete. My lungs burned and my legs felt like they were attached to cement blocks after about a mile and a half. The crew, riding in the cars, encouraged me to stop. Floyd told me to tune them out. He pushed me to go on when I thought I had nothing left. "Tasha, don't listen to them. Do you see that sign up there? Your daughter's waiting for you. If you don't make it, she's going to get hit by a car and die." I concentrated on his voice and tuned out anything negative I was hearing from everyone else. I was proud to complete three miles with him.

I realize his choice of words sound extreme, but he was sharing with me the urgency of maintaining my focus. I would need intense focus to deal with challenges that came my way as a result of working with this man.

Lesson 4: Take 2 Leave 1

My run with Floyd taught me an important lesson about how to become a champion. I've learned that who I surrounded myself with is critical to how far I will go in life. I realized there were three types of people climbing the ladder of success around me. There were people like Vivica, who were mentors reaching back to pull me up a rung. There were people like CeCe, who I looked out for, and reached out my hand to pull them up. They had my back and climbed with me. Then, there were the people, who were behind me wanting what I had, who kept trying to pull me down by my ankles. I had to shake them loose.

ROUND 5: BELOW THE BELT

Floyd had me in constant motion. I was part of his inner circle and the gate keeper to booking him exclusively for appearances and radio interviews on occasion. He probably made close to $500,000 from the appearances I booked for him from 2006 to 2008.

Promoters loved having him. Thankfully, he wasn't high maintenance when he showed up for gigs. Floyd never really had a strict rider like some other celebrities. He only asked for room temperature bottles of waters, cranberry and orange juice, and Red Vine candy. His dad forbade him from eating candy as a child. So, as an adult, he over indulged. I really should have secured him a Red Vine endorsement. Then again, knowing Floyd, he would have rejected the deal and tried to invent his own candy.

I mid-2006, we started to travel to Atlanta quite a bit for celebrity events. We flew there frequently, but the crazy thing was how we traveled to the city on this occasion. We were headed to the So So Def records weekend hosted by label CEO Jermaine Dupri and rapper Nelly. Floyd, one of his girlfriends, Angela, and the crew showed up at my house at midnight for an impromptu road trip. He probably wanted to drive to accommodate the 20 person entourage he brought on the trip.

Floyd, Angela and I drove in a twelve passenger van for about 38 hours. Another aspect of my job was to be the third wheel on a few of Floyd's dates, especially when he took them out for the first time. I've always had a gift for breaking the ice. Every ten hours Floyd sterilized himself with rubbing alcohol and baby wipes behind the van. He smelled like a hospital that had been sprayed with his favorite cologne, Issey Miyake. He probably shaved back there. Floyd hated, hated, hated hair on his body. He shaved everything from head to toe. Everything! I swore he had OCD.

He and Angela spent part of the drive recounting what they referred to as their "love story." I already heard secondhand about the infamous brawl between Angela and Josie. I got their version during that drive.

I was astonished that she still wanted to be involved with Floyd. She had suffered a beat down from Josie when she was leaving a club one night.

When Josie suspected that Floyd was cheating on her, she could get violent really quickly.

I don't condone the violence, but I understood where Josie was coming from. She was in love with someone who constantly disrespected her when he thought she wasn't looking. Josie beat Angela so badly that she broke her collarbone during the altercation. For the rest of her life, Angela's surgical scar served as a reminder of that fight and everyone involved.

Angela was behind the wheel for all but about six hours; and that's when Floyd drove. We could sleep when she was behind the wheel, but I had to stay awake when he was. I didn't drive at all. I rarely drove Floyd anywhere because the whole crew mocked me when I did. It wasn't that I couldn't, I've been driving since I was eleven. Everyone nodded and nervously smiled when I was behind the wheel. They were convinced that I couldn't drive and talk at the same time.

Despite this fact, Floyd let me drive all of his luxury cars back and forth from Vegas to Los Angeles while he was on *Dancing With the Stars*. He was fine with that. He teased, "I just don't trust you when somebody else is in the car." It was one of our running jokes.

When we finally made it to Atlanta, in the early morning, we had to dart to the Hartsfield Airport. Floyd was booked to appear on an episode of BET's long running *106 & Park* later that day. We took Angela and Philthy Rich artists Postaboy, Baggz, and HFLO to the show with us.

Although Floyd was the only invited guest to appear on the show, he was there to promote himself and the label. He insisted that his rappers walk out with him. I found myself in the middle of him and the producers trying to negotiate a group interview. Each time the answer was an emphatic, NO! The artists were mostly unknown, and the producers only wanted Floyd.

Floyd was unfazed and refused to schedule another time to have his rappers appear. It was now or never. When they called him out of the green room Postaboy, Baggz, and HFLO followed right behind him. Even though the producers were annoyed, they still invited us to come back to the show a few more times.

When we returned to Atlanta, the InterContinental didn't have rooms ready for our 20 person entourage.

I had to book all of us at the adjacent Embassy Suites while we waited.

I usually didn't have a room to myself when we traveled. Either I shared one with Tawanna, or I bunked with one of Floyd's dates. He never had the girl, or girls he traveled with stay with him. Even the ones who came for an overnight visit left their luggage in a separate room. Angela and I were supposed to be roommates through the So Def weekend, until she was forced to leave.

I don't know what happened between our arrival and the next day, but Floyd called my phone and instructed me to, "Put her on the next thing smoking." She had to be sent home immediately. Angela told me not to go through the trouble; she could book her own flight back.

I still didn't get my own room. Floyd's sisters Tawanna and Fannie showed up unannounced. I was surprised to see them since they were beefing with Floyd at the time. I didn't have a problem with adding more people to my room though. I wasn't one to get into family business, or come between siblings. Once Floyd knew they were in town he forgot whatever they were fighting about.

We were able to check into the InterContinental a day earlier than anticipated. Standing in the lobby, I shuffled through balance sheets from the Embassy Suites reconciling the cost from the block of rooms we reserved. I had the stack of papers in one hand, and my phone cupped between my shoulder and ear in the other. I was trying to get a status update on Floyd's cars. The Bentley, Rolls Royce and few of his other luxury vehicles were being shipped from Vegas just for the weekend. People I knew from Atlanta were annoyed. They joked with me, "How are you gonna let your boy come here and disrespect us like this, flossing all of his cars?"

With the exception of Josie, I never knew him to spend too much time being upset after a break-up. He always moved on so fast that by the time we left the hotel lobby he was already courting another woman, Shantel Jackson. He spit his game, but she rejected his normal "let me take you shopping" pitch. I think that surprised him. Floyd was like a girl's best friend. He loved to watch movies, shop in expensive stores, and eat at fancy fine dining restaurants.

Nelly discovered Shantel during one of his Miss Apple Bottoms Jeans model searches. Coincidentally,

Nelly also knew Melissia Brim, the mother of Floyd's oldest daughter, Iyanna. Nelly and Melissia were both from St. Louis.

Floyd had been about flossing and spending since I first met him. Any time I got in his ear to be more practical, he reminded me that it was his money and could spend it anyway he pleased.

He was pleased to let his money rain at strip clubs. Of course we hit up one while we were in Atlanta. Floyd's Louis Vuitton money bag was pregnant with $20,000 to $30,000 to shower the strippers. The song *Make it Rain* by Lil Wayne was the theme song that he'd drop his cash to. He loved himself some strippers.

When we traveled, there were at least three of them accompanying him. The way he treated the strippers was similar to how kings summoned jesters to entertain them. The only difference was Floyd didn't part with some of his entertainment at the end of the night. I often witnessed him telling girls to get dressed in the middle of their shift. He paid them to get off the pole and sit next to him for the night.

They were pawns in his private game of chess. I guess in a way, we were all pawns, doing exactly what he said. He affirmed this when he was interviewed by the well-respected writer, Thomas Houser, "I call the shots. Everything that goes my way isn't always the right way. I know that. But, I like things the way I like them."

Angela was in the strip club that night too. She was definitely resourceful. She managed to get a promoter to sponsor the rest of her trip. Holding a clear glass of something red and icy, she raised it up in our direction. Floyd nodded back as a competitor would when his opponent made a smart move against him. I obliged him when he asked me to bring her over to VIP. The next day, he had me send her some perfume to her room. At the same time, he was checking for Shantel hardcore.

Atlanta was my old stomping ground and I ran into people I knew all of the time. When I saw my old friends Eddie Weathers and Jermaine "JD" Dupri, Floyd attempted to introduce me to them. JD waited for him to finish before informing Floyd of our history. "Yeah, Tasha's my girl. We go way back." I knew that JD's stature as CEO of So So Def validated my history in the music industry for Floyd.

We weren't in town for a Mayweather weekend, but promoters took notice of the crowds and level of attention Floyd attracted anywhere he went. He was definitely entertaining. When we got home, there was a noticeable increase in the amount of requests I took from people wanting to book him for parties all over the country.

About a week after the So So Def event, Floyd flew Shantel in to stay at his house in Vegas. This was the first time I was formally introduced to her. She was pretty, though not yet the curvy bombshell that Floyd eventually molded her to be. Floyd definitely had a type, he liked the pretty ones and Shantel's exotic looks fit the bill. Her long locks framed the deeply embedded dimples on both sides of her face. I encouraged her to smile more often. Her dimples were adorable. She was also very quiet and oddly enough seemed to be unhappy. Most couples have a honeymoon stage when they first meet. I didn't see any signs that this relationship was new, or exciting to Shantel.

This was not at all the type of woman I was used to seeing around Floyd. Most of his women were confident and very extroverted. Her arms were folded most of the time and she barely spoke above a whisper. Her speech was slightly impeded by the braces affixed to the insides of her teeth. After she told me she wanted to go home within a day of her visit, I was certain that Floyd was going to send her back to Miami early.

Instead, her disenchantment was a challenge to him. It encouraged him to try to impress her more. It annoyed me, but I had already been admonished for telling him how to spend his money.

Shantel accepted his gifts as Floyd was obsessed with getting her attention. He barely knew anything about this girl, and still bought her a new Jeep before she left town. I don't remember seeing a genuine show of gratitude on her face.

I was involved with his work as much as I was involved with his personal business. He knew that I had a connection to Rozanda "Chilli" Thomas from the group TLC. Kevin was previously a dancer with the group. Floyd had a crush on her from the first time he saw TLC perform Red Light Special during their pre-show sound check in Grand Rapids when he was a teenager. I thought his crush was cute, but I wasn't convinced I should make a connection. Chilli wasn't receptive at first either. She said he was in great shape, and politely declined my invitation to one of his birthday parties.

She only changed her mind when I invited her as a paid guest to a charity event we were hosting in Grand Rapids. She agreed to come, but mentioned she felt uncomfortable being paid for the appearance. I made her accept the fee anyway.

Chilli didn't need Floyd's money, she had her own fortune. If he wanted to date her, he would have to do so by leading with his personality in a genuine way. He met her expectations early on. She was impressed by how he interacted with his children and gave Floyd a second look. The two of them made plans to reconnect once he got settled back in Vegas.

He tried to impress her although he still slipped up every now and then. During her visit he tried to park his Maybach in a handicap spot. She refused to get out of the car. I watched her admonish him from the backseat. "You are a gifted athlete. Why would you prevent a disabled person from parking here?" She demanded that he moved the car immediately.

When we all went to Cabo, she let me know that she was a lady even though she and Floyd stayed in the same room. He spared no expense. Their room at the Esperanza had a full sized swimming pool. Chilli was used to first class accommodations and Floyd made sure he provided them for her. She placed more value on how he treated her and those around him. She had a sweet nurturing spirit and I saw her genuinely try to get to know him on a deeper level. Floyd tried to keep her interested, but I wasn't surprised when they decided to keep their relationship platonic.

Not even a week after our trip to Cabo with Chilli, we ran into R&B singer Keyshia Cole in Miami. She and Floyd had been friendly since I invited her to his birthday party earlier that year. Coincidentally, it was the same birthday party that I tried to invite Chilli to. Keyshia's manager, Manny Halley, was a business associate of mine. They happened to be in Vegas that weekend and stopped by to visit Floyd. Keyshia and Floyd hit it off, but I could never tell if they had a romantic relationship or not.

Keyshia was a boss. She let Floyd know that she could hold her own on all levels. They had this weird rivalry type of chemistry to the extent that they had to be separated during a heated discussion about who was the better rapper, Biggie, or Tupac. Floyd was team Biggie. Keyshia was team Pac.

I got to know her better on a trip to Cancun, Mexico. She was really down to earth, just a normal girl with dreams and fears like the rest of us. Keyshia grew up in Oakland. She could be as sweet as pie, but nobody was going to punk her. When it was time to fly back from Cancun, Floyd informed me that we had to fly back commercial. He needed to take his jet to a business meeting. Keyshia interjected, "No, we're not. We came here on a private jet, we're leaving on one. I have my own." She told Floyd that she had seats for me and Tawanna too.

Their relationship remained friendly after that trip. I could still call her for anything. When we found ourselves in a bind to book an act for a fundraiser for St. Jude's Children's Hospital later that summer, Keyshia really saved the day. The Floyd Mayweather Foundation co-sponsored a gala with Red Rock Realty at the Wynn Resort on the Vegas Strip. We had Ashanti confirmed until she dropped out. I thought Keyshia was a better fit anyway.

She agreed to be our headliner at the last minute. In my haste to get her booked, she ended up in a middle seat in coach. The event was well under way and about to wrap up when she arrived. She was pissed. After only singing her platinum hit *Love*, she put the mic back on the stand and ended her set. Floyd made me pay her the $20,000 he promised out of my own pocket. Thankfully, Kevin and I mostly kept our bills separate. We didn't pool our incomes like other married couples. He would have hit the roof if he found out.

Working made it easier to avoid arguments with Kevin. He would go out during the week and not return until the next morning. Once I started finding loose phone numbers in his pants, I assumed he was cheating on me. This was our pattern. We'd have a couple of good months and then we'd be at each other's throats again.

Working for Floyd Mayweather was a paradox of great rewards and great consequences. I didn't know it at the time, but I treated Floyd's philandering like it was normal behavior. I didn't turn a blind eye to it, I knew what was happening. He wasn't my brother, or my husband. He was a young unmarried man. Furthermore, these women knew they weren't in exclusive relationships. I did tell him, "Somebody's going to break your heart one day."

This is why I had to forgive Kevin and stay committed to our relationship. If I didn't I would have been a hypocrite. I started to realize that I couldn't look the other way when it came to Floyd, and persecute Kevin at the same time. As much as his infidelity hurt me, my laser focus on Floyd hurt and sometimes humiliated him. To my husband I was having an emotional affair, and that was equally as harmful as physical infidelity.

Kevin wasn't intimidated by Floyd per se, he recognized that there were materialistic things that he couldn't give me, and to see Floyd do so deeply bothered him. As his wife, I should've recognized this and gave my husband greater emotional support.

Lesson 5: Detours In The Details

When anything is under construction, following the road signs will take you through the detour. A closer examination of the details of my work life allowed me to see where I was veering off course. When I started working for Floyd again, delays in making adjustments on my part had the potential to result in disastrous consequences. The first detour was the shift in how much of my time I gave to Floyd, and how much I allocated to Kevin. Ideally, I wouldn't have to see the same signs multiple times in order to make better career and life decisions.

ROUND 6: FUNCTIONAL DYSFUNCTION

I grew up loving the smell of a Michigan summer. Sometimes that included a day with the lingering scent of a rain-drenched backyard. Sometimes it included my grandma's cornbread made with farm-fresh corn. When my adult life got complicated, I yearned for that kind of simplicity. I was yearning for it during the summer of 2006.

My mom called me close to 3:00 in the morning. She asked me where the Spearmint Rhino strip club was. We needed to go there. My younger brother Kahil had been shot. I didn't process what I heard. I didn't feel anything. I just called the one person I knew who could tell me the address of the Spearmint Rhino.

Floyd took the call from his limo. Coincidentally, he was pulling into the parking lot there. He was out for the night with his then undercover girl, Shantel Jackson. Floyd was still technically with Josie.

He nicknamed Shantel, Miss Jackson, causing eyebrows to be raised from Tawanna and me. She was at least ten years younger than both of us. Needless to say, I never took to calling her anything besides Shantel.

Floyd was asking why I needed to be at a strip club at that time of night when his voice suddenly became stressed. Before I could tell him why I was asking, he blurted out, "Tasha, don't come up here. Somebody was murdered." Just like that, Floyd was the first person to tell me that Kahil had died.

My little brother was everybody's friend. He didn't hang with one particular click. Much like me, he could relate to all types of people. He was a kind, loving soul, and his death tore a hole in my heart that could never be replaced. We took comfort in knowing that a part of him would live on in Xia, and Seniya, the two beautiful children he left behind.

In the days that followed, arrangements needed to be made for my out-of-town family. For as much a disruption as Floyd could be to my family life, he was also incredibly generous. He wasn't the obvious choice for a go-to person when it came to help for my brother. Suffice it to say, Kahil and Lawrence tolerated

Floyd mainly because I worked for him. They respected him as a boxer, but didn't much care for the show that Floyd put on. They thought he was phony. Then, there was the infamous rap battle between TLO, an artist my brothers were friends with, and Dirt Bomb, the first rapper signed to Philthy Rich.

TLO slayed Dirt Bomb in a freestyle rap off. It wasn't so much that TLO was a better rapper because Dirty was a damn good lyricist. He lost because he didn't follow the rules of freestyle. His raps were supposed to be off the dome, not written and definitely not rehearsed. It was obvious to everybody, especially to Tawanna. If it was a freestyle battle; Floyd wouldn't have been able to recite Dirt Bombs lyrics. Tawanna busted them and let her brother have it.

Tawanna was and is as real as they come. She can be a little in your face, but once you know her it would be obvious that her bark is way bigger than her bite. I don't think her intention ever was to embarrass her brother and his crew. She voiced what all of us were thinking. Unfortunately, hurt feelings escalated to the point that one of Floyd's supporters took it upon himself to flash a gun from his waistband. I pulled my brothers out of there immediately.

From that day on, Kahil, Low, and Floyd were resentful of one another. However, their relationship took a slightly more amicable turn in July of 2006. Floyd and I were taking a flight back from Atlanta. It was one of the few times we traveled without the entourage. Out of the blue he asserted, "Your brothers are cool guys. You need to keep them out of the streets, especially the younger one." Kahil and Floyd had run into each other in a custom-made suits shop across town. Apparently, their short visit on neutral turf had allowed them to come close to making peace.

Floyd stopped by the house daily, but made it clear that he wouldn't be at Kahil's services. He repeatedly told me that he was willing to help in any way. Some of my Michigan family would not have been able to attend the funeral if Floyd hadn't stepped in and paid for a significant amount of the airfares. Until now, only Floyd and I knew how much he helped out.

The day after Kahil was murdered; Floyd called me to open the studio. I had the only key at the time. Several of his family members were extremely upset with him about that. He could have easily sent someone to pick up the key from me.

My life was surreal. I didn't allow myself to cry. I

had to be strong for the family. I walked around smiling at people all the time. Going to the studio was the only normal act that I had been able to accomplish in 24 hours. I not only wanted to go, I needed to go.

Floyd needed to meet me there too. He could have stopped by the house. Instead, he pulled rank as my boss. Before I opened the door, he made some wisecrack about me looking all jacked up. He sat me down to find out how I was doing, and asked for details on the condition of the body. He wanted to know if I'd seen the corpse and where Kahil had been shot. Then, he flat out told me that they were never going to catch the men who murdered my brother. I thought his questions were incredibly insensitive.

Judging Floyd Mayweather for how he grieved for my brother would be like judging a five-year old. I had come to learn that he didn't process things like most people. That's probably a true statement about how he lived his life as well.

In the ensuing days, he shared with me that a childhood friend of his has also recently been murdered. My brother's death forced him to finally accept the loss of someone he loved like a blood relative. We sobbed together without any explanation for a long time. Yes, the lines were often blurred between my work and personal life. This was one of the rare times when I was thankful for that blur.

A few weeks after Shantel left Las Vegas, I was still in the throes of sadness over Kahil's death. Floyd commented, "You're different since you lost your brother." He was right. I looked at life as much more fragile and fleeting than I did before. I experienced traumatic flashbacks when I heard loud noises. I damn near tripped on the hard concrete, and busted my head at the sound of a car crash, while walking in a Target parking lot.

My heart was broken. I was under a cloud of grief that I didn't know how to process. I needed to get moving again. Either Floyd sensed that I could use a distraction, or he was oblivious to the timing when he asked me to take a trip with him to visit Shantel in Miami. His motivation didn't matter. I needed a change of scenery.

I hopped on the plane, leaving my family to support one another during my absence. Kevin went back to work at his job with the telecommunications company. I think we all needed to fall back into a routine again.

When we got to Miami, Shantel picked us up in the Jeep Floyd bought for her. She was taking us to meet her family.

Her dad's house was nice and welcoming. There were pictures of her and her two brothers fishing on the wall. We sat down for small talk when her dad started asking her what her plans were for college. She politely obliged, "I'm going to do a couple of other things right now. Maybe some modeling." Her dad wasn't impressed. He was being the protective father when Floyd rudely interjected, "She doesn't have to worry about that. She's with me." Her dad shot back ignoring Floyd while addressing his daughter, "What happens when someone younger and prettier comes along?" There was awkward silence. I swallowed my beverage extra hard. I know if some guy came into my daddy's house interrupting him, we would have had a problem.

Floyd's daughter Iyanna was with us on this trip. I had a bond with his little girl from the time she was an infant. It began when Floyd trusted me to break her fever and care for her when she was sick.

She was the same age as my niece Xia. They would play together when I kept Iyanna at my house in Vegas. Being on the road with Iyanna made me miss my own two kids even more. I took extra special care of her.

I made sure she was in my room when we traveled. I wanted to protect her from witnessing any adult behavior, or conversations that she didn't need to be part of. I didn't like the fact that Floyd introduced her to women he was interested in so soon after meeting them. He did that a lot. If his mom or sisters weren't around, I kept Iyanna close to me.

I tried getting to know Shantel better while we were in Miami. During one of our conversations she shockingly admitted that she didn't much care to be around children. She most definitely didn't want any. I was certain that whatever they had going on would be short-lived. Floyd was a hands-on father to Iyanna and his other three children Jirah, Koraun, and Zion. They were always around.

Floyd's relationship with Shantel was whatever it was. I mean, I never really got it. He definitely wanted to feature her in public, but he would move mountains when Josie came around.

When Josie and the kids were visiting from California, he put Shantel up in a hotel down the street from his house. It wasn't anything fancy. He mainly wanted her close by. For years, he had me go over to his house and collect any signs that another woman had been there. I just came to accept this as part of my job. Even when he wasn't officially in a relationship with Josie, he didn't want her to know he was seeing anyone.

There's no way that Shantel didn't know she was being shifted out of the house while another woman visited. She had to fish her clothes out of her luggage in the trunk of Floyd's car every morning. I remember standing in his kitchen watching her casually stroll by wearing his white fluffy robe towards the garage.

I was going over foundation paperwork with my girlfriend Lana and just shaking my head. Lana was the Foundation's Secretary at the time, and in disbelief of Shantel's routine. I had already witnessed this foolishness before. When she came back into the house with fresh clothes in her hand, and headed back into the bedroom, we couldn't believe Floyd had her so in check. It was obvious that he was making sure Shantel's belongings were not in the house in case Josie popped up.

As a woman, I found it sad to watch Floyd act like he owned her. She was his prized possession. To me, it didn't seem like she was enough for him. He always had another woman in the background. He once told me, "I built Miss Jackson from the ground up. She ain't ever gonna leave me." I knew exactly what he meant. He gave her a full makeover from her physical appearance to her bank account. He completely upgraded her lifestyle.

Shantel was whoever Floyd wanted her to be. She seemed to be fine with giving explicit control over to a man that wasn't all the way hers. I could never understand why she chose to do so.

Given the foundation of their relationship, I wasn't surprised at the tone of their breakup in the spring of 2014. They had separated way before it became public knowledge through social meida. Still, Floyd crossed the line and blasted her on Twitter for allegedly terminating a pregnancy. I was puzzled that she even put herself in a position to get pregnant.

Floyd continued to fly Shantel to meet him wherever he was working. We were on the road a lot that year. In November, right around when Floyd announced his mega fight with Oscar De La Hoya, we were in Grand Rapids, doing some advance work for a Mayweather Weekend. This fight was a game changer for Floyd's boxing career and my work with him as a brand.

The fight was easily going to be his biggest payday of his career. Win or lose, he stood to earn upwards of $25 million. He strongly believed that he would beat Oscar. He had been telling anyone who would listen that he was definitely going to win the fight. He was looking forward to the huge promotional tour planned to market the fight as well. In the boxing world, he was living up to his self-created character as the villain, *Money May*weather. I wanted to balance his vibrato with a philanthropic side.

When we scheduled the Mayweather Weekend in the winter of 2006, I convinced Floyd to partner charitable events with our marketing efforts. There was a turkey drive, a comedy show, and a concert headlined by Young Jeezy.

We set-up shop at the Holiday Inn Express. It was a non-descript hotel that we could book and completely feel at home. Celebrities who traveled with us had to stay there too. A few years later, we bought out the entire hotel. I know the general manager was relieved that she didn't have to field calls from upset guests any longer. Especially since local Grand Rapids DJs Head and Buscat would spin in the lobby until Floyd went to bed.

Kevin's brother Aaron called me shortly after we arrived in Grand Rapids. Their father had passed away and the family wanted me to tell Kevin. Damn, I really wanted to be there to support my husband. I did the next best thing and called my dad and brother Lo to be present when he heard news from me. We never referred to each other's parents as "in-laws." The way we looked at it, family was family. Kevin called my father Dad, and Daddy called him Son.

I let Floyd know I had to leave immediately. He gave me his credit card to purchase plane tickets for Kevin and me to get to Atlanta. I was able to use the bonus money I made that weekend to pitch in on the funeral arrangements.

Instead of staying in Atlanta, after the funeral, I left, secure in knowing that Kevin was with his siblings. I returned to Michigan to finish up my work and got there in time for the concert we were promoting at the Orbit Room.

I watched the show from the side of the stage with

Floyd's "play cousin" Shorty. For some reason, he was clinging to me that night. He was telling me, "I really wanted you to work for Floyd again. I'm the one who got you your job back." It was strange for him to say that and walk away.

I could tell people were tense backstage. When I heard voices escalating, I followed the sounds to the green room to see what was going on. Shorty and Floyd's real cousin, Dejuan, were in a violent fight, crashing into the walls and turning over furniture. Someone shouted for Floyd to "shoot" Shorty! Once I saw a gun sitting on a cocktail table, I was like "hell no" and got out of there.

It got worse before we left. There was a shooting in the parking lot. It was a mind-numbingly freezing night in Michigan, I'd just buried my father-in-law, and I walked right into the middle of life-threatening chaos. My head was spinning.

At Floyd's orders, Shorty wasn't allowed to come into the hotel. I wondered what the hell was going on. Shorty and Floyd grew up together. They were inseparable. Now he was banished?

We finally were able to get some one-on-one time, and Floyd brought me up to speed. I knew Shorty had been jailed on drug charges then abruptly released. Ever since then, people had been trying to tell Floyd that he was a police informant. That weekend someone brought Floyd an actual copy of the deposition stating that Shorty gave police information in exchange for his freedom.

Floyd was teary-eyed angry. He felt betrayed and called him a "snitch." There were people who wanted to kill Shorty. Any of us could have been collateral damage.

I called Kevin to let him know there was drama, but didn't get into specifics. I still needed to be there one more day while we wrapped up payment to vendors. We cancelled the comedy show so we could leave Michigan early.

Tawanna and I had a little party in my room. I drank a lot. I was so drunk, I ended up dry heaving while Dejuan and Tawanna brought me a garbage can, and a cold rag for my face.

Floyd kicked everybody out to let me get some rest. He made sure I had my own security camped out in front of my room. I'd spent most of that year taking care of other people. That night was the first time in months that someone had taken care of me.

I never told Kevin about how I had to duck and cover a few times while on the road. One time in particular, Floyd was a financial backer for one of Lil Wayne's tours that Keyshia was also performing with. She came to visit Floyd after the show in Cleveland.

I went to my room early that night. I was half asleep when I picked up a call from Floyd after midnight. He ordered me out of bed telling me we had to leave immediately. He hollered, "Do not lay back down! Meet Keyshia out front! We have to go right now!" Fortunately, my bag hadn't been fully unpacked. My hair was still tightly wrapped in a sleeping scarf when I rushed to meet our chauffer waiting in the hotel's valet.

Floyd called me when we got in the car. "Tasha, don't worry. Have Wellington drop Keyshia and her girl off at their hotel." Once we did, Wellington drove me to meet up with Floyd and his security guards in Detroit. We flew back to Vegas the next day.

From what I found out, there was an issue with a dude that Floyd claimed owed him money. He never told me the complete details. All I knew was we had to get the fuck out of Cleveland and we were out!

Lesson 6: Deflection Can Be A Boomerang

There were early signs of dysfunction in my work environment. I didn't recognize them right away. In fact, the dysfunction started to feel normal. I have become somewhat of an inner-work junkie. Spending time with myself to sit with the praise and take the medicine has given me more peace than I've had in my entire life. What I put out into the world will eventually come back.

I've learned that running from my problems ultimately caused me to go in circles and eventually encounter them again. Though, it's been difficult to swallow the medicine, and then wait for it to work, the process has freed me. It's important to deflect less and use challenges as an opportunity to shine.

ROUND 7: WORK SPOUSE

The 2007 promotional tour for Floyd's fight with De La Hoya was one of the most entertaining boxing events in recent years. Floyd knew the fight was going to sell a lot of tickets; he wanted to push pay-per-view sales into record breaking territory. During our stop in Los Angeles, Floyd came up with the idea to bring a live chicken to the press event on Hollywood Boulevard. He had been calling Oscar a chicken and all kinds of names since the fight was announced. One of his security guards was from L.A. and knew where to find one.

At the end of his scheduled time of the mic, Floyd said, "Bring him on up. Bring Oscar up here." A caged chicken wearing a medallion engraved with the name *Oscar* was brought to the stage. The cage had a plate on the top that read *Golden Girl*. The already largely pro De La Hoya crowd booed even louder.

The May 5, 2007, welterweight title fight was the highest grossing in boxing history, posting over $130 million in revenue. Floyd's victory improved his record to 38-0, and I had my feelers out to contacts in the entertainment world. He was undeniably a boxing icon and had a persona to match his athletic skills.

My good friend and business associate, Tony Miller of All Axxess Entertainment, proposed a reality show based on Floyd and Philthy Rich Records. His contacts with VH-1 scheduled a meeting at the Red Rock hotel in Vegas. The show had the potential to create multiple spin-offs, and the exposure was an easy and inexpensive way to market our artists. We wouldn't have needed to invest any of Floyd's money to market our music:

Floyd disappointed me and Tony and killed the deal by insisting that the show focus completely on him. "Just turn the cameras on me, he professed. That's all they need to do." At the time, VH1 was a music/entertainment driven network and following him around uncut didn't fit their programming. Now that I think about it, he was probably ahead of their vision by about five years.

Life wasn't all work; there was a lot of pleasure. After we left Tony, Floyd asked me to meet him at Fletcher Jones Mercedes. I had to stop by his house and pick up his checkbook along the way. He collected cars like they were toys. He had purchased at least thirty cars by this time.

Rex, his personal salesman at the dealership met me at my Jeep and asked me for my driver's license. I was half answering Rex's questions since I was on the phone catching up with Teka. "Mine or Floyd's? I don't have his license on me." "Yes, yours, Tasha. Your boss just bought you a brand new Mercedes," he assured me.

I quickly ended my call with Teka. I was genuinely touched that he noticed how hard I was working. I thanked him repeatedly. I was overwhelmed with gratitude. "You deserve something nice," he professed. He wanted me to drive something that was a reflection of him. Floyd was flossy and according to him, I needed to be too.

I was in and out of the house so much that I didn't notice that Kevin had stopped wearing his wedding ring. He took it off eight months prior after a fight about something I didn't even remember anymore. Not wearing his band made him feel less married to me, I suppose. Ironically, wearing mine made me feel less married to him. It was one of the few tangible symbols of my connection to my "work husband," Floyd Mayweather.

I didn't coin that phrase, but it is applicable here. Working with Floyd was demanding. I was on the clock upwards of fourteen hours a day. Sometimes I felt like I was doing 24 hour shifts. I was immersed in his business and his up and down personal life, much like I was for Kevin.

When someone mentioned to me the concept of work wives and work husbands, I saw a parallel to my own experience. A work spouse is a co-worker with whom you share connections similar to those that would be shared in a marriage. There's loyalty and a bond there without the commitment and swearing before God.

You also do things for your work spouse that you might never think to do for your real husband or wife—like hide their secrets and make excuses for poor behavior. You might also be inclined to see your work spouse as much more interesting and deserving than the one you're legally married to.

I went with Floyd everywhere, whether it was a work related, or not. It wasn't unusual for me to visit his personal jeweler. I picked things up for him, and every now and then we'd go to the store together. On one particular occasion Floyd was buying gifts for himself and a few of his lady friends. I was trying on a white gold, diamond encrusted Cartier watch for him, which was not unusual either. He used my wrist for sizing items for other women before. They were mostly women who had other men in their lives who also bought them big-ticket items. Floyd courted the girlfriends of "ballers" like it was a competition.

When I was trying on the watches, Floyd mentioned I should get my wedding ring cleaned. I didn't want to leave the store without it, but we were pressed for time. Floyd assured me that he would have Jack pick everything up and deliver my ring straight to the house.

Jack, was Floyd's cousin, who sometimes filled the role of his personal assistant. When he came back to the house, he walked right passed me with the bags in his hands. He went into Floyd's bedroom and came right back out. On his way to the kitchen Jack mentioned, "Champ wants you to go in there."

Floyd was seated in the lounge section of his palatial bedroom holding a few of the jewelry boxes. He handed me the one containing princess cut diamond earrings. He always made jokes that mine were cubic zirconium, so he replaced them. I casually slipped my ring on when he handed me another box. I was still awestruck by the earrings he gave me. The next box was even more spectacular. He bought me the Cartier watch I tried on in the store.

Man, that watch was gorgeous! Kevin would flip out if I walked in the house iced up with over $100,000 of jewelry that Floyd bought. I planned to show them one at a time over the course of a couple of weeks.

"You didn't even notice," he chided. Floyd motioned for me to take a closer look at my left hand. Holy shit! He'd switched out the stone. Instead of the four smaller diamonds Kevin bought for me, the setting now featured a bigger and more stunning $10,000 rock.

Kevin gave me Chanel earrings and a new car before. He gave me what was within his means, but he wasn't able to buy gifts like Floyd was. I was astonished. I was vulnerable, and by this time, I was completely co-dependent on the lifestyle and escape that working for Floyd had given me.

I was experiencing a swirl of emotions. I was angry

that Floyd altered my wedding ring. I had anxiety over what Kevin was going to say. Then, there was where I landed. I allowed myself to accept the jewelry because gifts and attention from Floyd made me feel special. It had been a while since I'd felt that way at home. These gifts were carrots that got rid of some of the guilt I felt from working so many hours. They also deodorized the stench of the corrosive environment Floyd created for me to work in.

He made it a point to say, "I never bought anyone a Cartier watch. Everyone else gets a Rolex." I brushed it off because I watched him give expensive gifts to people he barely knew for years.

This had a lot to do with maintaining the "Money Mayweather" image; it was a form of window dressing. From the clothes we wore, to the cars that we drove, he wanted people around him to look a certain way because we were a reflection of him. I figured this was my shine.

Kevin and I had used our rings as both a wedge and bridge for a long time. Specifically, I've had to pawn jewelry, including my own wedding ring for both of them. I can't even count the amount of times I've had to pawn jewelry that Floyd gave me. Other times I did it to pay a bill collector without Kevin knowing. When Floyd was having cash flow issues, I pawned diamond earrings to cover some of his outstanding bills because I felt like I owed it to him.

That's why it was no big deal for me to pawn the jewelry he gave me. They didn't mean that much from the start.

Lesson 7: Peace of Mind Starts With Peace of Heart

I've learned that everyone has a story to tell and it's only human to feel hurt and disappointment. I was caught up in my emotions when Floyd gave me expensive jewelry, and those emotions tremendously clouded my judgment. When we use intellect to guide our decisions and inform the emotion of our story, the narrative is much clearer. Peace of mind can be obtained when you feel secure in your primary relationships, whether that is your spouse, closest friends, or family. Clear your heart in order to clear your mind.

ROUND 8: ROLL WITH THE PUNCHES

I needed to hire a new assistant in 2008. Tawanna was my road dog when we traveled and put on special events. She took care of business details like making flight and ground transportation arrangements for the large groups that accompanied us. She also tried to keep Floyd grounded. "Ya'll spending too much money," she let her brother know on more than one occasion. I agreed with Tawanna on Floyd's over spending.

Even when we were on shopping sprees I made it known that I preferred cash over gifts any day of the week. Floyd had urged me to start piling up items of clothing on his tab. "Tasha, get a pair of boots and a couple of outfits. C'mon, girl get whatever you want." I sat down in the middle of the store and told him, "I'd rather have my bills paid than leave out of here with some boots, Floyd."

His security would laugh, all the while complaining to me in confidence that they were sideways on some bills because Floyd wasn't paying them consistently. They watched him throw bundles of money away, sometimes literally, while some team members were struggling. This infuriated many in the Mayweather camp.

When Tawanna wasn't available, I was the only female working with Floyd.

She didn't work for me though. I needed someone to assist with my day-to-day duties. A young college student named Brandy was a perfect fit. I met her while I was working a Mayweather weekend in Grand Rapids. She was about to graduate from Western Michigan University with a degree in business. Her persistence in contacting me for an internship, reminded me of myself while I was at LaFace.

I paid her $250 a week to intern with me while she finished school. I really needed her to organize my email and keep track of the many voice messages I was getting requesting Floyd's time. She excelled at logistics; keeping my schedule and maintaining important contact information. Once she graduated, I relocated her to Vegas and doubled her weekly salary. Brandy was supposed to live with my family until Floyd could get her moved into a condo he was in the process of renovating. I had to maintain my commitment to her because Floyd only paid her sporadically, despite his promises.

After an unexpected call from Tawanna, Brandy's first official day on the job easily could have been her last. I was worried that she was going to pack up her things and head back to Michigan after Tawanna called me sobbing hysterically the day after she first reported to work. "What's wrong Tawanna? I can't understand you!" I was concerned because Tawanna wasn't the hysterical type. She wailed that her Uncle Pop wasn't breathing. She hadn't called the ambulance yet. I was the first person she called after she found him upright on her mom's couch.

I calmly told her to call 911 and wait for me and Brandy to get there. Within minutes, she phoned back to say go to the hospital instead. Pop had already passed away. I assured Brandy that even though our working environment was unusual, these were extreme circumstances.

I got to know Uncle Tony "Pop" Sinclair through Tawanna. Floyd and Pop understandably had an estranged relationship for most of his life. At the age of two, Floyd was used as a shield between his father and the shotgun of his Uncle Pop. According to the police report, the two men had argued at a roller skating rink earlier in the evening. When Pop came to the apartment to extend the confrontation, "Big Floyd" held his son and wouldn't put him down. That didn't slow Pop's determined anger. He shot him in the leg anyway. The shooting changed Floyd's relationship with his uncle for most of his life. Fortunately, they reconciled not long before his death.

I was always cool with Pop. He had this fearlessness about him that made him one of my favorite uncles from Floyd's family. When we drove back from L.A. after Floyd received his second *Fighter of the Year Award*, he wanted to make a pit-stop at Buffalo Bills. "Y'all pull into Buffalo Bills at the state line. Let's ride the roller coaster." So, we all did.

Pop was an amazing chef. The man could burn for real. On our trip back, he reminded me of the buttery, lip-smacking, crab legs he whipped up while I was pregnant with KJ. He was going to make them again that week.

Floyd never made it to the hospital. He was out of town with Tawanna's son Devaughn. When he arrived at his mom's house, he snapped at the rest of us coldly, "I don't know why ya'll are crying so much. He's in a better place." I was dumbfounded by his callous demeanor.

Brandy's introduction to her new work environment was like baptism by fire. She had a steep learning curve and had to work hard and fast to straighten it out. Her organizational skills and attention to detail got a lot of monkeys off my back right away. It didn't take long for me to trust her with a significant business responsibility.

My boy Chaka, whom I met in college, managed platinum selling artist Ludacris. Chaka knew I was working with Floyd and reached out to see if he wanted to be featured on Luda's track *Undisputed*. The song had a boxing theme and they wanted Floyd to be the voice of Luda's trainer. Coincidentally, Floyd and I were already in Atlanta celebrating his birthday. He took Luda up on his offer to record in his home studio right away. Floyd was a pro in the booth and knocked out his part in a little over an hour.

When the time came to discuss compensation, Floyd asked, "They're your people right? It's all good." Even more surprising, when Chaka wanted to film the video in Vegas and use the Mayweather boxing gym,

Floyd eagerly agreed to participate. He even suggested they use a couple of his cars in the video.

The day of Luda's video shoot, I got a call from Steve Rifkind's associate wanting to schedule a meeting with our group Kolour Blind. Steve was the Founder and CEO of SRC records and was Vice-President of Universal/Motown when he signed Akon.

Word got to him that Floyd started an R&B record label, and signed a new group out of Nashville. Kolour Blind was a diverse male R&B quartette that Kevin and Aaron had been co-managing. One of the group members was actually blind. Steve was interested in hearing more, and got my contact information. He wanted me to bring the group to audition at his home in Los Angeles. Since I couldn't be in two places at once, I left Brandy in charge of the video shoot.

When Chaka asked me to get a final tally from Floyd regarding his appearance fee and the use of the location, Floyd didn't charge them a dime. This was huge. I looked out for people, and in turn they looked out for me.

People like Steve Rifkind don't call you every day. How I structured my team helped me work more efficiently. I got more accomplished and was able to make more strategic moves. I was truly the right hand to the champ. When people wanted to do business with Floyd, they called me.

Lesson 8: Your Network Is Your Net Worth

One of my earliest lessons in business was given to me by Davette Singletary when I worked at LaFace. She taught me the importance of maintaining a network of key contacts. Knowing people wasn't as important as exceeding their expectations. The money came and went. The respect I spent years earning amongst my colleagues proved more valuable than any amount of money Floyd could spend.

ROUND 9: 3 COMMA JOE

By the end of 2008, Floyd Mayweather was the second-highest earning athlete in the world, according to *Forbes* magazine. He ranked higher than Kobe Bryant, LeBron James, and tennis great Roger Federer. Only Tiger Woods—a man with his own well-chronicled, self-inflicted turmoil—was ahead of him.

Floyd's $65 million was earned almost entirely in the ring. The man had taken enormous risks with his body, and the risks paid off in huge financial dividends. At the same time, he has also taken enormous risks with his money. Some of those risks have had disastrous consequences.

The biggest of these missteps involved a man we called, 3 Comma Joe. Floyd named him that because he was a billionaire. At least that's what Joe wanted us to believe. We met him after Floyd's retirement in 2008. We were on the road with *WrestleMania XXIV*, doing quite pre-event publicity for the March 30th bout with Paul "Big Show" Wight. One of our scheduled stops took us to New York City about a month prior to the actual match. That's where I met a man named JT.

JT was really vague about what he wanted. He gave me his card and conveyed he had a business opportunity he wanted to discuss with Floyd. That happened quite a bit. People pitched all sorts of business ideas for me to bring to Floyd.

My job was to present opportunities to Floyd and allow him to decide what he wanted to do, not to turn them down. I never wanted to be one of those gate keepers who kept their boss from things they didn't want to hear. I wasn't making my own side money either by working out a deal first, and then try to sell it to Floyd. To some other people it was all about what they could get out of it before they even took the opportunity to Floyd. I felt that if I was fair to him, he would be fair to me.

We didn't have time to meet with JT while in New York. I asked him to get back in touch in a couple of weeks once Floyd was done with his *WrestleMania* obligation. I also wanted another chance to hear him out. It wasn't clear to me what he was proposing.

JT called me about a month later. This time he got

straight to the point. His exact words were, "I want to show Floyd how to become a billionaire." Floyd envisioned himself as a billionaire in the next few years. I knew he'd at least be interested in knowing what JT's plan was.

JT was proposing a cash-trading program. It involved pooling large sums of money from a group of individuals and flipping the cash to significantly increase everyone's investment. According to JT, this was relatively risk free. More importantly, he vouched it was legal.

He went on to explain that if Floyd put a certain amount of "seed" money into an escrow account, he could grow his initial investment and be paid back on a biweekly basis. Floyd's response to setting up a meeting with JT was," Hell yeah, I want to meet this dude."

Since I was never in the position of business advisor, I asked him specifically if I should call Leonard. I didn't want to step on anybody's toes. Floyd was adamant that he didn't want anyone else, especially not Leonard, to know about this deal.

He understood, or claimed to understand, what JT was talking about in half the time it took me to get clarity. These two spent a few more weeks talking about the plan and otherwise establishing a working relationship. I had my own responsibilities to handle and stayed out of the day-to-day negotiations between Floyd and JT.

JT arranged for Floyd to sit down with two investors in the trading program. Steve was a multimillionaire, and Bill was supposed to be a billionaire as a result of his involvement. Of course, Floyd wanted to meet Bill. He was already a multimillionaire and didn't have much use for Steve's endorsement.

We were all set to meet Bill. Instead, in walked Joe whom we soon dubbed "3 Comma Joe," since he alleged to be a billionaire. Joe was a man JT claimed he didn't even know. He was this slick talking man with perfectly coiffed sandy brown hair. He looked like he was in his mid to late 40s. He sat down at the table with his blond arm candy ready to make a deal. This guy was Floyd's kind of flashy. He claimed to have piloted one of his three jets for this meeting.

They got down to business quickly, and before I knew it, Floyd's signature was bleeding all over everything. There wasn't a lawyer present, no business advisors, and no time to back out. I tried to tell him to slow down and get his personal attorney and even Leonard involved. He declined. "I got this, Tasha," he brushed me back. He committed to giving Joe $15 million on the spot. In return, Floyd was supposed to earn $5 billion in the trading program. At Joe's advisement, Floyd was to deal exclusively with his Canadian attorney.

Early on, Floyd was getting his money back in one million dollar increments on a biweekly basis. He and Joe spent a lot of time together while Joe convinced Floyd of the viability of the program.

Floyd was so certain this money was real that he allowed me to do things with the business that hadn't been possible before. I could finally hire a team to help me run Mayweather Music.

We hired Grammy award winning producer, Shannon Sanders to produce the song *Sorry* for Kolour Blind. Our next act was Tilly Key, a French born powerhouse R&B singer. Vagaz brought her to Floyd's attention after watching a few of her YouTube videos. Tilly's experience included working with renowned producers Jimmy Jam and Terry Lewis as well as the Avila Brothers. These acts had the vocal ability to become stars. Things were finally moving in the right direction for the label.

After knocking out Ricky Hatton in December of 2007, Floyd's record improved to 39-0, and he announced his retirement from boxing. The deal with 3 Comma Joe along with the projected success of Mayweather Music, made it more likely he'd stay out of the ring for good this time.

To commemorate Floyd's retirement, we planned a Mayweather weekend in Grand Rapids. Floyd has a lot of love for his hometown. He knew that all of his friends and family couldn't make it out to Vegas. So, he took the Vegas life to them. I arrived with my team ahead of Floyd while he stayed behind to finish up editing *Round 13*, a documentary of his life that the public was allowed to purchase tickets to view.

The three-day celebration featured events all around Grand Rapids. Beschelle, our foundation's executive director, worked out an arrangement with the City to host a carnival downtown. I facilitated several celebrity driven events which included a bowling bash, one of Floyd's favorite group activities. We scheduled an all-white movie premiere of *Round 13* and flew in a custom made *Money* green carpet for celebrity arrivals.

Since Floyd grew up going to roller skating rinks in Grand Rapids, we bought out a rink and invited the public to skate with Vivica A. Fox, Taraji P. Henson, and Regina King amongst others.

We hired Keyshia Cole and Lil' John to headline a star studded concert which also featured Tank, Ray J, and Trey Songz. It was like we landed on Boardwalk with a grip of Monopoly money. He gave me a generous bonus that I used to make investments and to secure my family. We were living a dream. Three months later, it turned into a nightmare. A 3 Comma Joe nightmare.

Joe stopped returning phone calls, and the money train came to an abrupt halt. Nobody could find Joe, and no one could find Floyd's money. Not the $15 million and definitely not the $5 billion. Life in the Mayweather camp got really nasty for everybody.

When Joe got in the wind with Floyd's money, he affected other revenue streams as well. Bill collectors were calling and I was becoming the queen of deflection. Floyd wasn't able to control his agitation. He beckoned me, "Where the fuck is Joe with my money, Tasha?" He wasn't hollering at me. He knew I didn't know where Joe was, he was just frustrated and needed to vent.

My nerves were raw too. I was getting an earful from Floyd and trying to manage other business obligations. He didn't want to book any club appearances. When we received deposits, he started pulling no shows. Understandably, his missing $15 million had him on edge.

The 3 Comma Joe situation was a problem. Our problems came in threes too. Floyd stopped honoring his promotional commitments. While we were trying to track down Joe, promotional gigs became a quick way to get cash in hand. The walls were closing in on Floyd, and I was walking on eggshells trying to cope with his mood swings.

JNICE was one of the promoters who sent a deposit of $12,500, half of the total booking. He wanted his money back. I could tell he didn't want friction with Floyd. This was just one opportunity; he could book him elsewhere at a later date. He needed to get money back to his business partners. If it weren't for our friendship things could have gotten heated really fast.

Mike Deniro was the second promoter Floyd stiffed for an appearance commitment. We met him at the So So Def weekend we attended in Atlanta. Mike was an understanding guy, but definitely a businessman.

He booked Floyd for a major Obama inauguration party in D.C. Mike's event was an opportunity to earn some positive P.R. due to the fallout from a private meeting a few months earlier. Lana and I were instrumental in arranging for Floyd to have a 20 minute one-on-one with then candidate Obama. Subsequently, members of the media questioned Floyd's connection to a Las Vegas fundraiser.

He was disinterested in anything political even if it wasn't an official inauguration party. Many well-known Black celebrities were in D. C. It would've been a great photo opportunity for Floyd. Contrarily, Leonard stepped in, "Floyd has both Democrat and Republican fans." I was so irritated with Leonard's interference.

Mike wired the money into my account. I immediately gave the entire deposit to Floyd. Once he got the money, he changed his mind. "Tasha let them know I'm going to send the money back. I'm not doing the date." I was pissed that he backed out. We were already in the red with JNICE, and now Mike. Floyd used his dad's hospitalization as a reason to renege on the commitment. Mike accepted his excuse because he said he would have made the same decision. He just wanted his money returned.

I let a day or two go by before asking him to send back the deposit. I didn't want to press him too hard, but we were driving to the bank anyway. I looked out the window while he took a phone call from rapper, and nemesis T.I. "Yes, I called Tiny," he screamed into the phone. "I was talking with her about promoting shows and maybe you would be interested in doing business. What? You know where I am? Ain't nobody trying to fuck your bitch!" Floyd hollered and hung up on him. He wasn't in the mood to discuss much after that.

The weekend passed and Floyd was ignoring my requests to get the money back. Mike called again to get a status update. Fed up with the excuses I was giving, he snapped, "Tasha, why is this dude out here spending thousands on purses and jewelry for women and I can't get my money!" Now he had bass in his throat. He knew what was up and I couldn't lie to him.

I knew real recognized real. I told him straight up, "Look, he is having some financial issues and on my word he will pay you that money back." The only value I could offer Mike was my word. That meant everything to me in business.

It took about two weeks for me to clear the books to these promoters. They both continue to do business with Floyd to this day.

The last straw involved a promoter out of Charlotte named Shonda. She and her partners booked Floyd for two dates in New Orleans during *NBA All Star Weekend*. Although all of my conversations were with Rhonda, the paperwork was signed by her partners. Within a day of making the deposit of $12,500, Floyd had a meeting with Shane McMahon from the WWE. We realized the All Star Weekend conflicted with a WWE promotional date. He wouldn't be able to travel to New Orleans. I was in the room with Shane, Floyd, and Leonard when I called Shonda to decline the deal. Floyd agreed to send her money right back.

She needed to call her partners before agreeing to anything on the phone. When she got back to me, she said Floyd could keep the funds because they already printed up promotional items using his likeness. According to her, we were even. When the WWE tour stopped in NYC, Leonard condescendingly told me that we were being sued for not making that appearance in New Orleans. His tone insinuated that somehow it was my fault.

I was perplexed because I spoke to Shonda before we landed. I was planning to meet with her while we were there. She assured us that her partners had acted alone in the lawsuit. I was surprised to find out they settled out of court.

I didn't think Floyd would need to come out of pocket like that because I could prove we were told to keep the money. When I challenged Floyd to press Leonard on the issue, I was dismissed like I didn't know what I was talking about. For the first time, I felt like just a girl.

Things got really thick inside the Mayweather camp. My integrity was questioned too. Leonard and I bumped heads because he felt I was responsible for some of Floyd's problems. Especially since he was up to speed on what transpired between Floyd and Joe. Floyd contacted the SEC and the FBI. I was instructed to give a deposition on everything I knew about the agreement.

Floyd directed me to give all of my notes over to the authorities. I didn't hesitate because I knew I took impeccable records down to the keeping a proper call log. Of course I maintained all the email and documented the details of every meeting I attended with them.

The longer Joe stayed out of reach, the greater the distance grew between me and Floyd.

Lesson 9: Beware Of The Boss-Friend

Once the 3 Comma Joe deal went south, I was clear that I was working for Floyd Mayweather and not working with him. In business you either have a boss, or you have a friend. A friend can be a mentor and a straight shooter who lets you in on trade secrets. A boss signs your checks and has the luxury to shift accountability at will. You can never have both at the same time.

ROUND 10: COLY

Floyd's money woes started to seep into every aspect of his life. In addition to the secret we were trying to contain about 3 Comma Joe, we now had another issue. I was told that the IRS had filed a petition to freeze Floyd's assets until he settled an outstanding $6 million in back taxes. Our monthly trips came to a halt and shopping sprees were out of the question.

It wasn't like we didn't have other deals on the table. There were offers which included everything from reality shows to feature films, but we were stalled. Floyd didn't want to move on them. Without immediate access to cash, his quality of life was affected. We were flying coach while Floyd settled back fees with a private jet company we did business with. It was as if he wasn't comfortable in his own skin. Without money to showboat with, he practically went into hiding.

The most noticeable casualty of the cash flow

problem was the very thing he could control, which was his own behavior. I'd been around Floyd for a long time, and we'd been through a whole hell of a lot. I had never seen him so despondent.

This situation was exacerbated by the fact that he desperately wanted to move. He moved a lot and in the twelve years I was working with him, Floyd changed residences seven times.

He had greater cause to move in August of 2008, when burglars slipped into his guarded, gated community and made off with $7 million in custom-made jewelry. More than the invasion of his home and theft of his possessions, it was a personal violation.

I was at Applebee's taking a meeting with my assistant, Brandy, and our label consultant, Ian Burke. Even though Mayweather Music was without cash, we weren't without the will to grow the business. Brandy was giving an update when I answered Floyd's call, hoping he only had a quick question. "Tasha, Tasha," he was yelling, "Do you know what this bitch did?"

Floyd calling and yelling wasn't anything new. Floyd calling and yelling the word bitch incessantly was. When he said it, I knew he was heated. It was common knowledge that he had a problem with people even jokingly calling a woman by that name. Even when I used it in jest to refer to myself, he would correct me, saying, "Is that what you think of yourself?" Honestly, it always made me feel kind of stupid because he was right.

He was hollering so loudly into the phone that I had to take the call away from the table. Even though I asked him several times, he couldn't tell me what was going on. He needed me to come to his house right away. This was so typical of how we operated. I'd start to make progress on the business front only to be called away to address Floyd's personal life.

Ian and Brandy rode with me. I had to take them to Floyd's home ASAP without giving them any details. I asked them to wait in the car while I went in to see what was going on. I didn't want them to see him so out of control. I at least, had to stay composed. Floyd was pacing the floor of his home theater in front of Coly, one of the women he'd been seeing for a little while. My instincts were correct. We had a serious problem.

They looked like they hadn't slept in a week. Coly was sunken into the infamous Mayweather massage chair. She was barefoot and barely covered with a wrinkled sweater dress. Her shoulder-length, dark blond, hair, was tussled all over her head. Coly hadn't ever been a mess like this; at least not in front of me. This is significant because Floyd called her the sexy one, as she was always so put together. I never heard him talk like that about any of his other women. I mean he would use words like *pretty* or *cool*, or say this or that one has *that fire*. He'd never say, *sexy*.

He couldn't stand still and was screaming, "Tasha, she put my life in danger." I was thinking she did something out in the streets to jeopardize his safety. Nothing he said made sense to me. I did manage to piece together that somehow it had gotten back to Floyd that Coly had been seen with her ex-boyfriend. This was a big no-no. Even though he could have as many chicks on the side as he wanted, none of *them* were allowed to see other men. Especially not this one.

There was probably more heat on the situation because the two of them had history and had dated a few years prior. According to Floyd, he rescued her from a man who was abusing her at the time. I can tell you it meant something to him to have her back in his life. He bought her a car, set her up in a beautifully furnished condo, and filled the closets with expensive clothes. As if that weren't enough, he invested $30,000 into a clothing store she was about to open.

After listening to her side of the story, I ran through a pattern of behavior that unfolded over the course of about five months. It started when she mistakenly pocket-dialed my phone. She was talking to another man which was disrespectful of Floyd. The whole conversation was recorded on my voicemail. When I shared the message with Floyd, he turned a deaf ear to the whole thing. He just dismissed what I told him.

At the time of the jewelry robbery, Coly didn't give her full legal name to the cops. Her decision caused friction in his family. Floyd also wanted phone records from everyone who was in the house that day. He wanted a list created for himself to do his own investigation. He instructed me to create the list by asking everyone to disclose their phone log. That list included Tawanna and her son Devaughn.

Tawanna was furious that Floyd even put her name on the list as if she was a suspect. Floyd wasn't accusing her of anything. He didn't want to overlook the fact that someone she may have spoken to that day might have set him up. He was paranoid.

Tawanna stopped speaking to me for a while after that incident. Eventually, she realized I was only following orders.

A few months later, Coly claimed someone stole an expensive ring Floyd gave her. Shortly after that, a pair of $50,000 earrings inadvertently was flushed down the toilet. She also happened to be in the home the day of the jewelry heist. All of her expensive jewelry loss occurred at the height of Floyd's money issues.

Floyd wrung his hands, explaining that he went "raw" on this chick. That's what he meant by her putting his life in danger. He was convinced that she was also having sex with her ex-boyfriend. He was a clean freak germaphobe, and the thought of having seconds repulsed him.

After about an hour, I had to get out of there and send Brandy and Ian home with my car. They gave me a familiar look of both frustration and understanding. We'd lost at least a day's work, again.

When I returned to the theater room, Floyd was still pacing and hollering incoherently. He instructed his security guards to camp out in front of the door. In the room, Floyd was very domineering. I was now not only concerned for his state of mind, I was growing concerned that this woman was being held against her will.

He taunted her to try to leave. She appeared to be frightened and confused. He threatened to cut off all of her hair, and let the crew take turns with her. Coly didn't say anything. She kept her eyes fixed on the floor. We were in a circular argument that kept branching, and branching. I pulled Floyd aside and told him to try to calm down. He had to let Coly go home if that's what she wanted to do. I asked her if she wanted to leave too. Both of them made it clear they were fine, so I left.

I sent Brandy and Ian off in my car hours ago. I ended up driving one of Floyd's SUVs home to my family. I hoped he would clear his head overnight. We had business at stake and possibly another legal situation if he didn't let Coly leave the house. My head hurt and my body ached for sleep. I collapsed into my bed around 4:00 a.m. only to be awakened by a call from a friend of mine. It was in response to the text messages I sent that afternoon. My suspicions were confirmed. Coly was definitely involved with other men.

I'm pretty certain I drove back to his house in the same clothes I wore the night before. This time I was the one doing the yelling.

Floyd, Coly, and one of the security guards were all asleep on the floor in the theater room. He preferred not to sleep in the bedroom since the robbery. Thinking about how she had violated our family made me angry. The next thing I knew, Floyd was trying to pull me off of her.

I hate that I was so out of control. Kevin and I have argued many times that Floyd's personality was affecting mine. He tried to get me to see that the chaos had become normal fare. Perhaps it had. Consequently, I couldn't turn it on and off.

Instead of Floyd putting Coly out and siding with me, he made excuses for the situation. "I have everything under control. I know everything, he stated." I seriously thought the man had completely lost his mind. He went from one hundred to zero, being extremely calm. Coly seemed comfortable and compliant as well. Shit was real weird. I threw my hands up and walked out of the house.

I was hotter than fish grease when he called me. He could have taken another day or so, and I still would have been fuming. He didn't even come close to apologizing to me. He wanted something. The request was for me to get the title to Coly's car; he was going to have it signed over to me. My response to this was, "absolutely not."

I didn't care that Coly's car was nicer and a newer model than the Mercedes he bought for me. If he wanted to upgrade my car, he could have done that. He wanted to take something from Coly more than he wanted to give something to me. He switched up like that, giving and taking from people. It was part of his need for control. I didn't want any part of that B.S.

He had a second part to the plan. He was taking matters into his own hands in the search for 3 Comma Joe. He was taking Coly, Jack, and a small security detail on a long drive through Seattle into Canada to surprise Joe's attorney. I was to fly to Seattle and join them on the drive from there. Floyd was so combustible that I was convinced I needed to go to keep an eye on him.

I didn't even explain this trip to Kevin. What was I going to tell him? "Hi, honey. Floyd's making Coly drive us across the border to collect $15 million." I called my mom and asked her to help out with the kids. Sometimes I asked for forgiveness instead of permission. Besides, I had a stake in getting Floyd's money back. I wasn't being paid while this problem was being resolved.

When I arrived in the Seattle hotel room, they were all in a holding pattern. The security guards and I had already witnessed the blowup between Floyd and Coly. None of us knew what to say when we learned Floyd was going to let her drive everyone across the border. This was insane. I took Floyd into the bedroom for a sidebar. I wasn't getting in the car with this woman before I had an explanation. I didn't feel right about what went down in Vegas.

However, being a woman I knew how we can flip the script and snap. Some of this was on him, and some of it was on her. I was uneasy and distrustful of the situation. Especially since we were about to transport her across the border into another country. She could have driven us all off a cliff somewhere.

Floyd's plan was to use Coly as a decoy. He had information that Joe was going to be visiting his attorney. Instead of him and a bunch of intimidating black men knocking on the door, Coly was going to do it. "Besides," he added, "she damn near looks white and can blend into a lot of places we can't. She has the complexion for the connection." My sleep deprivation led me to believe this was a viable plan. Neither Joe, nor his attorney had been picking up or returning calls for a couple of months.

Things didn't go so smoothly at the attorney's office. We waited in the lobby for a few minutes only to be told Joe wasn't expected that day. The attorney was visibly nervous. There were two 250-pound security guards in the lobby, and he was eye to eye with the best boxer in the world.

Floyd told him that we had driven all the way from Las Vegas and weren't leaving until Joe was on the phone. Instead of calling him from the room, the attorney excused himself to use another phone, leaving his cell on the conference table. It seemed like he left it there on purpose. As soon as that door closed, we dove for it and copied all of Joe's information. When the attorney came back into the room, of course he said Joe didn't answer the phone when he called.

We almost got stopped on our way back into the country when the Canadian border agent questioned Coly's expired passport. In my haste to get out of town, I grabbed the wrong one from her condo. Coly was street smart. After explaining that she was on a business trip with Floyd Mayweather, they let us cross. The border agent happened to be a boxing fan.

Back in town, there was still the lingering Coly issue. She had to go home. We were all so cordial on the trip that I thought maybe Floyd was going to work it out with her. Not so much. We got back to his house and were there just long enough for him to shower. He came out of the bathroom as if he'd washed off any remaining civility he had for her, and emerged a different person. His hot and cold behavior was very close to being manic depressive.

He was ready for Coly to leave; only she wasn't going to stay in the condo anymore. Two carloads of us went with him to evict her. I road with security in an SUV, while Coly and Floyd rode together in his Maybach. The group of us remained silent when Floyd went with her upstairs. I assumed she was going to pack a few bags. She had a lot of clothes and other belongings in that condo.

When they came back downstairs, all she had was the clothes on her back, a bra, and some panties clutched in her hands. She blinked away tears as she turned to us with a humiliated shrug, "I'm sorry you guys." He made her empty her purse in front of him. She looked away and walked out the door. He put her out on the street. I sympathized with her, and I pitied him. In fact, the whole situation was pitiful.

After she left, he callously looked around, "This is what happens. Jack, get this place cleaned up. Somebody else will be in here." Floyd wanted to drive me home from the condo. We didn't speak when we first got in the car. I sensed he was sad and hurt. I tried to break the ice and let him know that it was OK to feel those things after a break-up. I told him I would be there for him if he wanted to talk. He fumbled with his music and seemed to be ignoring me until he uttered, "I'm going to see my daughter when I drop you off. Thank you Tasha, for being a real friend."

He was within his rights to take his things back, but he wasn't within his rights to bully and intimate a woman. I realized my boss, my friend, wasn't the invincible champ; he was just a regular man with feelings. In this instance he was unstable and increasingly fragile.

Lesson 10: Losing Can Mean Winning

It's okay to simply walk away and not feel like you've lost, or have been defeated. Especially when you start doing crazy things that put yourself or your family at risk. In that very moment, choosing to lose anything unhealthy can mean that you've won. I learned to recognize when that happens and summon the courage to remove myself from the situation. There were plenty of times when I should have stood up for myself. I should have stood in my own conviction and told Floyd the things he didn't want to hear more often. I wouldn't stifle that again. Even if it meant my boss would have listened less, I would insist on starting there.

ROUND 11: THE RUBBER MATCH

Not long after we returned from Canada, I got a call from a female acquaintance of Joe. Somehow she got my number from snooping through his phone. Allegedly, Joe had become violent with this woman effectively ending their relationship. She was distraught to the point that she was willing to provide information that would lead us to find him. What's the phrase? "Hell hath no fury like a woman scorned." She was hoping Floyd would get his hands on Joe before the police did.

Floyd was able to follow up on a couple of locations she provided. One in particular led us to a boat. A boat named 3 Comma Joe. This guy had a sense of humor. A couple of deck hands knew of Joe though he hadn't been around in a while. The marina lead was another dead end.

Another dead end was a surprising call from Joe. Out of the blue he reached out to me. It wasn't peculiar that Joe was calling me instead of Floyd.

Business associates often called me when they wanted to get connect with Floyd. This was no different.

I got right to the point. I needed to know where the rest of the money was. He wanted Floyd to know there was money coming. He needed more time to address the death of a key business associate. According to Joe, the deceased individual was integral in securing the remaining money. I didn't believe a word he said.

I had this sinking feeling that Floyd was going to need to do something in order to make money. The only other option was to get back in the ring. Leonard had been pushing for this almost immediately after Floyd announced his retirement. Although boxing was an immediate solution to Floyd's financial problems, it wasn't an answer to his emotional state of mind. In my opinion, if Leonard cared about him, he would have tried harder to find other means of income outside of boxing. I was trying hard to be a team player. More importantly, I was team Floyd, while another key member was team *Money*.

Floyd had begun sending documents to both the SEC and FBI. We were hoping that the wire trail would lead investigators closer to anyone responsible for absconding with the cash. This was a real caper with a real villain. We got word that Joe colored his hair from blond to black and surrounded himself with security.

The longer Joe stayed out of reach, the greater the distance grew between me and Floyd. Some of the tension was clearly due to the lack of funds. Mayweather Music and the Floyd Mayweather Foundation were under my direct purview. Both of which were essentially closed operations.

Floyd didn't care much for discussion about the label since it all came back to the need for money. I had to figure out how to make progress without him. I tried to remain positive even though I felt like we were digging a ditch that would be impossible to climb out of. Thing started to fall apart.

Kolour Blind was released from their contract and we were in the process of doing the same for Tilly Key. Like so many of my dealings with Floyd, the Kolour Blind signing was personal. Kevin, managed the group, and it was painful, yet not new, for me to be caught between the man I loved and the man I worked for. We had already invested close to $250,000 in both of their projects and couldn't drop one single to show for it.

We couldn't pay any of the producers who worked with Tilly, or Kolour Blind. Consequentially, word started to circulate that Mayweather Music wasn't making good on its outstanding bills. For me, this wasn't completely about the label. I felt the weight of my own career sinking as well. My credibility was taking a hit, but I didn't hide. I took every call and gave people the best information I could.

Once the money flow stopped, Leonard took the opportunity to push me as far from the inner circle as he could. He blamed me for the 3 Comma Joe scam and convinced Floyd to come out of retirement.

What was I supposed to do? Pretend like it didn't happen? It was a brutal time during my personal and professional life.

Out of one side of Floyd's mouth he would tell me that it wasn't my fault; he made the decision to invest with Joe. His actions spoke louder than his words as he stopped following through with anything that I asked him to do. My workload was reduced to a trickle of online bill paying.

Lesson 11: Cross Check Your Double Check

I had access to an iconic athlete in a way very few people in the world could experience. He didn't wait until he had a fight on the books to prepare. He stayed ready. He woke up in fighting shape. He went to bed in fighting shape. Being ready for all things at all times was a best practice learned while working with Floyd.

I advised Brandy to create project wrap books after every event. We captured everything from venue contracts to press release clippings in hard cover binders. I had no idea keeping records this way would be such an important use of my time. It served me well when I was interviewed by the FBI.

ROUND 12: SPLIT DECISION

Tampa was unusually cold, even for late January. Even under pressure we looked fly. In this case, fly left us freezing. Open toe heels and flowing dresses weren't enough ammunition for the Central Floridian winter. I started to empathize with tourists back home who were taken by surprise that Las Vegas wasn't always sunny and sultry.

January 28, 2009, was two days before my birthday. I was close to kissing forty and still maintained a blossoming career as an entertainment industry executive. I had hoped the breakthrough would've come by now. At this point, I was unremittingly rubbing the pieces of my dream together like campfire flints. I was convinced that I could turn a bunch of sparks into a flame somehow.

We were but a small part of the hundreds of thousands that had descended upon the region to take part in *Super Bowl XLIII* pre-game events. The sports books had the Arizona Cardinals as underdogs to the

Pittsburgh Steelers. Though it wasn't written as such, we were underdogs as well. That's one of the bonds that kept me and Floyd Mayweather working together for 12 years. We were both underdogs.

In my heart of hearts, I knew we shouldn't have taken this trip. Mayweather Music was about to be a label without artists, or direction. These issues were dwarfed by the elephant in the room—the money. "Money" Mayweather had serious cash flow issues, and this trip was going to force me to scramble and create smokescreens in order to protect my boss's image.

I'd been scrambling for almost six months at this point. To the public, Floyd's money woes were primarily the result of a colossal outstanding tax bill of $6 million. The two of us knew what the world didn't: he was duped in a cash trading scam; scammed to the tune of $15 million. Assets were frozen everywhere.

Times were so tight that a couple of my own staff members came out of pocket to fund their travel in order to work in Tampa for the week. This was embarrassing, but we had to make this trip to collect a much needed check.

That too was complicated. My dad's cousin and one of his business associates wanted to create an unforgettable VIP Super Bowl event. *Champion's Ball* was to be a star studded party with celebrities, athletes, and musicians. The headliner was the Champ himself, Floyd Mayweather.

My team was involved mainly because Floyd needed the money. Also, I knew my cousin didn't have experience putting together celebrity events. I was straight up with everyone about the finances before they agreed to get on board. They still had my back.

When I say my team, there were certain individuals that stayed on through difficult times because they believed in me as much as I believed in them. Y'all know who you are and I love you dearly for holding me down when business activities slowed, and when the checks stopped.

The idea of a Super-Bowl party made sense to me from a marketing perspective. When he was on his game, nobody could out promote Floyd Mayweather. The offer of $60,000 was a lifeline to the reigning champ. This wasn't make-it-rain money. This was keep-the-lights-on and pay-the-private-school-tuition-of-his-four-kids money.

I sat in a two-room suite cramped with five other women all trying to pretend that we could contain the bleeding. We all covered for him to our significant others, business associates, and the public. None more than me, and I was about out of evasive maneuvers.

Others were starting to see firsthand what I had been desperately trying to conceal. He was coming undone. It was after 4:00 a.m and most of us needed to be awake and ready to leave at 5:30 a.m. for a scheduled appearance at Jim McMahon's Celebrity Golf challenge. Time to shower and get dressed was eaten up by a colossal argument between Floyd and Vagaz.

He rapidly banged on the door of our suite. When I opened it, he came running in with Big Bull and Vagaz right behind him. "Tasha, send her ass back on the next thing smoking," he shouted with rage. Brandy got out of her bed in case she had to book the flight. Vagaz was a crying mess. Her glasses dangled off of the bridge of her nose as she screamed back. Floyd was angry because Vagaz had gone to visit friends that were staying in another hotel. "I was with my friends. He thinks I ain't shit," she choked up looking in my direction. My girl Lana and I had to stand between them. I didn't know if Vagaz was going to swing on him. It was that heated.

There was something very disturbing about that argument. Vagaz looked traumatized, and she was trembling. I managed to defuse the situation and rushed Floyd and Big Bull out of the suite. Vagaz ended up in the closet of one of the bedrooms curled up in a fetal position.

"You don't know what goes on in that house," she sobbed inconsolably. She couldn't tell me or Lana exactly what she meant when we asked her to give more of an explanation. To this day, I still wonder what she was talking about. She left on a flight back home to Atlanta where she stayed for several months.

It wasn't until recently that I realized Tampa wasn't the beginning of the end. It was simply another beginning.

My working relationship with Floyd was over by April of 2009. I knew it was time for me to move on with the rest of my dignity.

To add insult to injury, he called Brandy and told her that she would be working directly for him. Personal feelings aside, I gave her the blueprint to Floyd's inner circle. At first, I wanted to hold her hand to help her navigate the landmines in his life, but I had to remind myself that I needed to rip off the band aid and let go. I was unemployed and exasperated.

Brandy had all of his key contacts. I made sure I didn't leave her out there like that. Almost everything I knew she knew as it pertained to Floyd's business. She knew where the checkbook was and how to contact his business associates. I put my personal feelings aside so that the transition would be seamless for Floyd. Even in my darkest days, I was still thinking of how to make his life easier.

I was in transition in every part of my life. Kevin and I were separated too. I had a shortened fuse from being worn out by taking care of Floyd and his problems. I turned into somebody that neither Kevin, nor I knew. I snapped and physically attacked him when I found more phone numbers in his pocket. We needed space. I moved out with KJ, Jaelin, and Brandy to a five bedroom house down the street from him.

I needed space from Floyd, but he was still reaching out to me. I got a series of late night calls from Floyd leading up the Marquez fight of September 2009. He wanted out of boxing. He simply didn't have the appetite for the sport that he once had. He had to change focus to his children. He repeated over and over, "Tasha, I gotta feed my kids. Everybody has to eat."

Inevitably, my time in the Mayweather camp came to an end, as all things do. I had my plan to make my way up the ranks and pay my dues as an entertainment professional. The master plan wasn't to work for Floyd indefinitely in order to achieve this.

Floyd has said on more than one occasion, "Tasha is with me forever, either I will bury her or she will, bury me." I took his words to be earnest, even sweet, until I heard him say the same thing about several other people. His words turned into a slick pickup line that no longer had any meaning to me.

Lesson 12: Get Out Of Survival Mode: LIVE

Roadways in the desert are most slippery when it starts to rain after a dry spell. All of the oil sits on the surface of the road causing them to be particularly dangerous when wet. Such is life. We're most susceptible to going off course during major topography changes of the heart. Every ounce of insecurity and raw emotion magnifies itself and forces reconciliation before we can move forward. I was tightly wound worrying about Floyd, his money, and how it impacted my life. I couldn't escape the worry long enough to create a plan of action for myself. Once I let go of survival mode I was able to breathe freely. Acknowledging self-doubts allowed me to learn that it's okay. It's okay to fall. It's okay to rise.

ROUND 13: PUNCH DRUNK

The first week of September 2010 was peculiar even by Floyd Mayweather standards. I was focused on my new business venture, Treasures Consignment Boutique. When we first opened I had a small salon attached to the business. The retail store featured gently, or never worn clothing, and accessories from my celebrity friends with really trendy new items. A portion of sales was being donated to local charities I had worked with for years. Floyd even gave some of his clothes to get me started.

Transitioning from being Floyd's right hand to taking charge of my own businesses was bumpy in the beginning. I still got calls from people wanting to pitch Floyd for one thing, or another. There wasn't a mass press release to announce my departure; people didn't know that I was no longer working for him.

I let him know we needed to talk about a new acting opportunity that was brought to me. A highly revered television producer wanted him to star in a hot new show. I thought it would be a good look for him to be cast as a character completely opposite of what the public knew him as.

When he picked me up the first thing he asked was, "Did you see the YouStream videos? I've been streaming for a couple of days." Mainstream media like ESPN and Yahoo Sports had converged on what was called a "racist and homophobic" rant directed at fellow boxer Manny Pacquiao. Floyd thought it was all a joke. "People forgot all about Tiger Woods, Tasha. They'll forget about this too," he bristled.

It was just like the old days. I had business to discuss and Floyd was distracted by some personal issues. I had to hear about his drama as he took me to the M Casino on the south side of the strip so he could place a bet. He took over the conversation and by the time he dropped me off back at my house, I never got to bring up the television show.

I gave it one more try a couple of days later. I stopped by his house hoping to finally share the television show opportunity with him. People were sitting around while Floyd was nowhere to be found. Sounds of laughter and music echoed off of the marble countertops and slate flooring. Finally, he called me to the living room to talk while he was getting a massage. We only got about halfway through the business before he got off the table and walked out of the room for no apparent reason.

I wasn't on his payroll anymore. I could leave whenever I wanted to. When I called his phones they rang from the nearby coffee table. I yelled his name up the stairs and still no reply. I couldn't find him. I couldn't call him. I went home.

After midnight, I saw several missed calls from him. I figured he was calling to apologize for not finishing our business. In the morning, there were reports that he was being sought for a mix of domestic violence, robbery, and grand larceny charges. He turned himself in to police on September 10. By late afternoon on September 11, Floyd called me after being held in jail for a few hours.

Honestly, I wasn't trying to be in his personal life anymore. I was his friend, and I was glad he was okay. When he first told me his side of the story, the incident didn't seem that serious to me. Josie had called the police on him before only to admit that she lied, so I didn't know what the real story was this time. I was at Treasures with a store full of customers when he called. I couldn't really give him my full attention. I figured the situation would resolve itself quickly. He didn't sound worried, so neither was I.

The media had a different take, and every outlet speculated on the seriousness of the matter. The reports and his attorney must've gotten into Floyd's head. His tone was different when I called him back that evening. I could tell he was alone.

"Tasha, I want you to write a few things down. You remember the suit I told you about? I want you to lay it on the bed. I want you to make sure to tell my kids that I love them. I'm coherent, Tasha. I know what I'm saying." The hours immediately after he was formally charged with eight crimes, including two felony counts of coercion for threatening to beat his son, revealed a sober, honest, Floyd Mayweather. He was losing hope.

He called to say that this time he might not be able to withstand the fall out. His relationship with Josie had been nothing but tumultuous. He wasn't so upset over the fact that the two of them were involved in yet another incident. Similar charges were dismissed in 2005, after Josie admitted she lied to the police. It was the involvement of his children that gave him so much grief. Floyd would do absolutely anything for his kids.

He asked me to meet him at his house after he made a few phone calls. He was being so cryptic that I grew more concerned by the minute. He wouldn't say whom he needed to make these final calls to and barely acknowledged me having asked him any questions. He was talking slow and deliberately. "She got my kids talking to the police. My kids!"

Our conversation was interrupted a few times, and he abruptly hung up. Even though his mood swings were thoroughly unpredictable under normal circumstances. I could tell that this time was different. It almost seemed as if he was coming to terms with his own perceived inevitable demise. My main focus was keeping him on the phone. I thought if I was talking to him, then at least he wasn't going to harm himself at that moment.

Like most people whose friends call them in crisis, I was in disbelief. I didn't know what to do. I had thoughts of calling his mom, my mom, and other family members. I also wanted to protect him. I didn't want to expose him in his current state of mind. What if he really just needed support? Getting everyone involved could only further isolate him in his own destructive thoughts. I'd seen him shut down before. I didn't want him to go there this time. My heart was racing, and I was afraid of what the outcome could be.

I kept telling him, "This is unnecessary. We can talk about this. Stop talking about your funeral." I really didn't want to go to his house alone and I tried not to. I called his sister and my girlfriend Lana to meet me there. Neither of them picked up the phone. Keep in mind I no longer worked for Floyd. I wasn't speaking to my boss. I was speaking to my friend, who was in a very bad place; which is why I ultimately drove over there unaccompanied.

When I arrived at his house, the front door was unlocked and slightly ajar. I was petrified. The only thing that moved me forward was the thought that I could stop him if he hadn't already done something to himself. "Floyd, where are you? You here, man?" I called out to him as I walked hoping to quickly find out that he was okay. The stillness was a stark contrast to the noise and commotion I'd encountered there a few days earlier. It creeped me out.

The truth is we'd been here before. Floyd talked in detail about his funeral several times over the years.

What he'd wear, what would be said, and even the position of his own body in the casket. The first conversation was in 2007. A videographer was recording our car trip to L.A. It was as if Floyd was telling us so his wishes would be carried out.

I had to ask him to turn off the camera more than once. I've known him long enough to confidently say that Floyd Mayweather doesn't want to live off camera. We kept rolling.

I had a nervous feeling in the pit of my stomach. I needed to see him breathing so I could hug him and then slap the shit out of him for worrying me like this. A few steps in, I found him. The house was 22,000 square feet, and all that mattered was the small space that his chair was situated in. He was alone and sitting in complete darkness. It was warm outside, but he always had the fireplace burning.

I experienced an earnest Floyd Mayweather. There was no bravado. No swagger. He sat prone, not really facing anything in particular with a pensive look on his face. He was reflective, and his tone was incredibly somber. "It's going to be over soon, Tasha. This will not end well."

Josie claimed that Floyd flew into a violent rage once he learned she was dating another man, stole her cell phone and beat her, in front of their children. Many public figures have made prescient statements as their lives have spiraled out of control. I wondered if this was his. If convicted of all eight charges, he faced up to 34 years in prison. That would qualify as not ending well.

I took a deep breath and leaned forward from my chair. "You're a champion, you don't give up. You need to stop this and go to counseling to get well." At this point I knew something was wrong, but I didn't think it was something me or anyone else could help him with. I truly felt he needed to see a professional. Nobody else from his inner circle ever told him to seek therapy, but this was not the first time that he had heard it from me. If he had a broken foot, I would tell him to see a specialist. The same was true for his broken thoughts. It took me years even to see it myself.

We talked mostly about our kids and families. He bludgeoned himself mercilessly by rehashing the fact that his son, Karoun, witnessed this incident. First, his father, then his Uncle Roger, and now Floyd himself was facing charges of domestic violence.

We sparred verbally for hours with the gloves off before he looked at me and simply exhaled. It was over. "I'm going to a movie. Thanks for coming by." He stood up, and we both walked out of the house.

I don't know if Floyd was suicidal or not. All I know is, when he rose up from his chair, my heart started to beat again. I had spent many years worrying about my friend and the damage he exposed himself to inside the ring and out. I was caught up in the character "Money Mayweather" and overlooked how unhealthy the man was.

In retrospect, I also overlooked how unhealthy I was. It was time for both of us to face the music and make changes in our lives.

Lesson 13: Most People Don't Change, But We All Evolve

I can't say that I've changed as a result of my experiences over the past twelve years. I'm still the same woman at my core. However, I have evolved. Knowing that about myself gives me the courage to face new obstacles along the way. Every time I've flinched "ouch" has resulted in learning how not to make the same mistake again.

UNDISPUTED CHAMP

I've learned that adversity is the purest form of truth. I've been able to get to the core of a problem faster when there was adversity involved. During the last week of June 2012, I experienced adversity magnified. My father summoned the family to meet at Kahil's gravesite. I know this sounds unusual, but this is where my father, mother, Lawrence and I met when we needed discuss something important.

My parents divorced for a second time a little over a year prior to our meeting. The memory of Kahil's life kept our family together. Sadly, the grief brought on by his death broke my mom and dad apart. It's not unusual for couples to split-up after losing a child. His passing was just too much for their relationship to overcome.

Daddy recently remarried, yet my parents were still close. I learned from my parents that the depth of a family's commitment went beyond romance. In the forty years that they had known one another, they had three children and divorced twice. They gave each other a whole lot of headaches and remained in each other's lives. Not for our sake, but because they were soul mates.

Driving into the cemetery, I had a knot in my stomach. The kind you get when you have a feeling of impending doom. My dad looked melancholy. He masked his emotions well enough. I could tell there was something wrong in the tone of his voice.

The four of us were having a casual conversation when Daddy sighed and let out, "Well guys, I have the big C." Cancer, he had lung cancer. Tears ran down mom and Low's faces, but none of us moved. My eyes filled with water until my vision was completely blurred. I was in disbelief. How could this be happening? My dad was the strongest man in the world to me and seemed far too young to be sick.

When my Papa passed after his three year battle with cancer, he was close to 80 years old. My father turned 60 in March of the year he was diagnosed. Like my grandfather, he still had an incredibly vibrant spirit. My daddy used to kick it! He was a fighter and this was a battle that our family would fight alongside of him.

I wasn't a fan of chemotherapy or radiation. They seemed too strong and made my Papa incredibly weaker when he had them. I researched homeopathic approaches and any sort of natural remedy that would heal the body. My great aunts from Chicago sent me herbal teas to give to Daddy.

We all went to his first oncologist appointment. During which, I pointedly asked, "What will happen if he didn't do chemo? How long would he live?" The doctor looked at my dad, but answered me, "Three months." "Really?" I responded. I thought to myself, no man not even a doctor, can tell me when my father was going to die. I wanted to fight for my dad. We opted for the chemo.

His first chemo treatment was scheduled in mid-July. He responded well. He remained very positive which was important to me. I read that when people were diagnosed with incurable illnesses, 80% of their healing process was attributed to their attitude. If this was the case, my dad's health was headed in the right direction. We were going to keep fighting.

When August rolled around, the treatment was taking its toll.

When I noticed his hair falling out, I bought him a fedora. He wore it the entire day. We were all pretty upbeat until we noticed his right hand didn't seem normal. It looked almost limp. A few days later he was hospitalized after being unable to move his entire right arm. My father had a minor stroke and didn't even know it. That's a Robinson-we keep pushing.

A CAT scan revealed that his brain was bleeding. The cancer had spread and I was terrified by the thought of losing my father.

I tried to keep a level head and go about my business somehow. I relocated Treasures Boutique a few weeks before my dad was diagnosed. Focusing on work and my children provided a light in the darkness my family was experiencing. Our eight year old son, KJ, was a budding superstar who we had to help direct his creative aspirations. He convinced a classmate to manage him and schedule daily lunchroom performances. KJ was especially known for his spot on Michael Jackson impersonations.

Kevin and I were also getting Jaelin ready for her junior year of high school. Her mind was set on applying to fashion college. I allowed her to work with me at my store to learn about the retail side of the industry.

I was at Treasures when Floyd called me having been released from jail after serving two months of his three-month sentence. I hadn't talked to him since before he got locked up due to his altercation with Josie. The most I may have said was hello through Melissia when he called her while we were working out. That was pretty much it.

He wanted to let me know that no matter what we had been through, we were friends, and I should have called him about my dad. It hadn't even occurred to me to call him. At that time, I felt closer to Melissia than him anyway.

He offered to help me financially in order to get my father the best treatment. His gesture was sweet and kind of strange at the same time.

I spent most of my time with my dad. Sleeping in the hospital chair one night, I turned over to see Kevin tucking him in. He took such care fixing the blankets and making daddy's bed comfortable with more pillows. My dad acknowledged Kevin's deed by giving him a fist bump. Their exchange was like my father walking me down the aisle, and giving me away to my husband in the wedding that we never had.

Although my father approved of me marrying Kevin, we missed out on that tradition in our drive-through ceremony. We were planning to renew our vows for our twentieth anniversary. Witnessing the tender way Kevin looked after the man who had taken such good care of me, put us back into a sacred place.

In some ways, the challenges that Kevin and I faced throughout our marriage served to bring us closer together. We bent a whole hell of a lot, but we didn't completely break. In one of my darkest moments he was my light, and the warmth he radiated reminded me that he was my soul mate.

On August 31st, 2012, we moved daddy to a hospice facility. There would be no more treatment. Family members took turns keeping vigil at this bedside. The men in our family really stepped up.

The morning of September 3rd I arrived at the hospital very early. Low and my cousins Christopher, Eon, and James were sprawled out across the room like they had a big boys sleep over. My cousin Demychael and my dad's first cousin Clyde made sure Daddy was washed up and changed his gown.

God bless hospice nurses. The women assigned to our case were empathetic and treated my dad with dignity. By the early evening, we were told to stay close by.

My mother came and left quickly. Watching Daddy's final moments were too much for her to take in. The two of them had known each other since they were 18 years old. Divorced or not, he would always be her husband. She would always be the love of his life.

My grandmother led us in a recitation of the Lord's Prayer. We held hands over him while listening to his gurgling lungs fill with fluid. He started to sound like he was making train engine noises. We all knew it could be any minute. The hospice nurse returned to check his vitals. There was silence. No more train sounds.

I screamed "Daddy!" at the top of my lungs as I heard him take in a long deep breath that sounded like "Yaah." He sat straight up, opened his eyes and scrolled the room. He looked at my brother Low and I and relaxed back into the bed. He exhaled, "Weh. He was gone. At 8:35 p.m., Daddy made his transition. Low held on to his hand for at least an hour after he passed. The swelling he had in his hands and feet went away. His face was no longer puffy either.

This was the first time I ever witnessed someone dying. I feel fortunate that I was there with my father. He brought me and my brothers into the world and we were with him when his spirit left his body.

I rushed out of the room to go see my mother. I didn't want her to be alone when she heard the news. This wasn't something I was going to say over the phone. We wept and held each other tightly. My mom always had great perspective. She wiped away both of our tears and declared, "The only way to heaven is to take off the flesh."

While the family and I were making funeral arrangements, Floyd called again. His concern seemed very genuine. He was friendly with my father and course Daddy enjoyed watching him box. Floyd even hired him to inspect a few of his properties. Daddy was the lead housing inspector for the Las Vegas Housing Authority.

He sent me a text to check my messages. I hadn't picked up his call in a couple of days. The voicemail expressed how much he cared for me and my family and to let him know if we needed anything. He would take care of it all. He was acting strange. I think he was even whispering.

I politely declined. I didn't want to accept money from Floyd ever again. I knew there would always be strings attached. Plus, I knew my father had money in his bank and a life insurance policy. I knew we could cover burial costs as a family. What I didn't know is that we needed it right then and there. Without receiving the death certificate, we couldn't get his life insurance money. Putting us in a deeper bind was the fact that a week before my dad's wife of less than one year emptied his bank account.

My brother owned a barbershop and was in the process of opening his restaurant, Soul Food Café. His money was tied up in those business deals. I was low on funds after relocating Treasures to the other side of town. I still didn't want to ask Floyd for money.

When the two of us spoke again, the problem we had with covering my dad's burial costs was resolved. A family member was going to float us the money, but we had to pay them back. Floyd offered to give me the money again. I turned him down, but he insisted we meet at Bank of America anyway. This was the first time I saw him since he was released from jail. I didn't know if incarceration changed him on the inside, but he looked different to me. The man I knew hated any sort of hair on his body. Floyd was now growing a goatee.

He handed me a cashier's check for $9,000. When I told him I didn't need that much money, he acted like he didn't hear me. I was fixated on giving it back to him back as soon as we got our insurance money.

Tony Miller and I booked Floyd for an appearance to host a party in Detroit in October. Floyd was to be paid $30,000 and his associate Ricki Brazil was to receive a commission. Out of the blue, Tony called me and asked me about a $9,000 balance to be added to the bill. Ricki called him to relay the message from Floyd. He didn't go into details. He said I would know the reason.

Floyd has this special skill which allows him to sense when people are vulnerable and in the most need. He offers them a hand and then snatches it away. It's a terrible game of bait and switch.

I was enraged! I didn't know we were engaging in a business deal when he gave me the money for my father's funeral. I thought he was genuinely a friend helping a friend. Smoke was coming out of my ears and I immediately called him.

It hadn't even been a full week after I buried my dad. Floyd called me for everything else. He chose to try and embarrass me by involving Tony. I told him he would get his money way before he went to Detroit and that he didn't have to play a cat and mouse game with me. He tried to back pedal by making the assumption that Tony knew he had given me the money. Why would Tony know? Even if he did, why have Ricki call?

Within a month of my dad's passing, I got a check from his life insurance policy. I was determined to pay Floyd back. I met up him and "Princess Love" his beauty of the *weak* at the Palms Casino. I handed him an envelope which had the $9,000 cashier's check inside of it. I wrote a memo that read "reimbursement."

I felt great that day. I paid him back and removed the debt from hanging over my head. I was sure Floyd didn't think I was going to pay him back. That's why he got Tony involved.

He's given a lot of money away; thrown it on the floor at people in some instances. He's paid for funerals of people he didn't even know. The value of our friendship came down to $9,000. I felt a sense of personal accomplishment that I could give him this money back. Not that he needed it. He was probably just going to waste it on a purse for Princess Love.

The money meant nothing to him. It meant evolution for me. It took me a while to get to the point where I saw my connection to Floyd Mayweather for what it was, a strange business arrangement.

When I went back to the bank to repay my cousin, I found out the IRS garnished my account. All of it! Five years after I stopped working with Floyd, a 1099 from Mayweather Promotions was sent to me. Hundreds of thousands of dollars were funneled in and out of my account for Mayweather related events. Promoters and clubs would pay me directly and I would give Floyd the money. I suppose this prevented Floyd from paying taxes on the money himself.

I didn't suspect that Floyd was directly involved in the 1099 because he didn't really handle any part of IRS reporting. He coldly responded that my bind wasn't his problem. I knew it wasn't his problem directly. It was a problem I let him create for me. I had to report upwards of $500,000 that he stashed in my accounts from appearances and other dealings.

I had to account for everything including wire payments for fight tickets for celebrities including Nelly, Ashanti, and others. I personally handed their tickets to their representative, and was instructed to give the money directly to Leonard. To the IRS it looked like I hadn't paid taxes on a half million dollars. So not true!

Even when Floyd prepaid for a bundle of advance tickets for his fight with Oscar De La Hoya, I had to charge my girlfriends Lana and Nicole $500 a seat. I assumed all along that Floyd would give some of his extra tickets away. I couldn't give them to Lana or Nicole since, "Every ticket had a price," according to Leonard. He insisted he had to charge them because he was holding tickets for people who didn't show up.

I escorted Nicole to the ATM so she could put the money in my hands. I had a job to do, but I hoped Floyd would reimburse them. I think Floyd was surprised that I even charged them in the first place. Especially Lana since she had been working with us that year getting the foundation off the ground.

The next day, he offered Lana her money back, but not Nicole. Ironically, Nicole now works directly for Leonard as an executive with Mayweather Promotions.

This was one of the worst money decisions I've ever made. Being paid under the table put me in a bad position with the IRS. I learned a really hard, cold lesson, and I won't ever do that again. It took me two years to clean up that outstanding debt.

Almost a year after my father passed, I decided to close Treasures. I needed to re-define my next steps. Fortunately, I could still count on my sisterhood to help me regroup. My dear girlfriends Christie, Stacia, Lana, CeCe and Tawanna showed up for the parties and for the funerals. My girls clapped when I got promoted and then extended those same hands when I needed help from the pavement.

My girlfriends were honest with me when they heard the bravado, "I'm doing just fine." They observed smooth movements while knowing that under the surface I was peddling like hell. They had my back. My girl Ebony, whom I had known since before we entered pre-K, invited me to join her on a trip to Paris. It was a work trip for her and I could tag along for some much needed R&R.

After my dad passed, she mailed me handwritten letter. The contents of that letter will remain between the two of us. I can say I will always be touched by the love and care she put into writing it to me. It's so important to me that I keep it in a safe place with KJ and Jaelin's birth certificates.

Being in Paris with Ebony made me think a lot about my life, what I had been through, and what I was going to do next. Any direction I was headed in would keep my family as my compass. Jaelin was accepted to the Fashion Institute of Design and Merchandising (FIDM) in San Diego. Kevin and I were so proud of the young lady she was becoming.

I was able to confront the pain I managed to suppress for years. At last, I gave myself permission to grieve my brother, papa, and daddy.

I reflected on my career. So much of my identity was wrapped up in my business and work with Floyd. A part of me died when those things ended. I decided to take my boutique online, shoot my reality show reel, *Tasha's Treasures*, and continue to raid my celebrity friend's closets for charity.

With the help of a counselor, I was able to open up and let go of the heaviness. I even began to understand myself and others more. I realized that everyone goes through things. I wanted to be defined by how I got through my challenges.

A week after my return from Paris, my brother Low was admitted to the hospital. He was in complete renal failure. Eighteen years prior, my mother donated her kidney to him, and it was shutting down. We didn't need to look far for another donor. I volunteered to be tested to see if I was a match. Extensive blood work revealed that my tissue wasn't compatible. Our family remains prayerful that we can find another match amongst ourselves. Meanwhile he remains on the national donor list.

Life truly is about the journey, not the destination. I haven't always ended up where I thought I was going. But, it's been a lot of fun trying to get there. I've realized that I've grown so much. I've made personal and professional mistakes and I embraced them. I've done things that made me wince, especially as I relived them on these pages.

I learned so many valuable lessons that encouraged me to write this book. It took me a long while to get to this point. My spiritual journey has really brought comfort to my life and things seem more transparent now than ever. I still care about what happens to Floyd Mayweather as a human being. I understand and am deeply perplexed by him at the same time. What's new is that I finally care more about what happens to Tasha Robinson-White.

17440235R00133

Made in the USA
San Bernardino, CA
12 December 2014